Contents

INTRODUCTION

There are some 8,600 bird species living in the world, of which more than half are 'songbirds' or passerines of the order Passeriformes. They form the most widespread bird group, occurring in all continents and almost all the habitats one can think of — from river banks and ponds to high mountains, from tropical forests and arid steppes to cold northern taigas and tundras. Like all bird groups, the order Passeriformes is characterized by certain more or less distinct features.

External and morphological features

The external features of songbirds, namely the body, beak and feet, the shape of wings and tail and the structure and colour of the feathers, are exceptionally varied. Nevertheless, some common characteristics can be distinguished. Fig. 1 shows the basic structure of a passerine's body and its individual parts.

In terms of size, songbirds vary from very small to medium-large birds; the two extremes are represented by the Goldcrest and the Firecrest, weighing 5 to 6 grams, and, at the other end of the scale, by the Raven, weighing approximately 1.2 kilograms.

The bill of a passerine or songbird is usually short or medium-long, lacking a cere (the bare area at the base of the bill seen in, for example, parrots and birds of prey) and varying in shape according to the type of food eaten: in seedeaters, the beak is conical and strong, often serrated and well-adapted for holding and crushing hard-covered seeds; in insectivorous birds, it is delicate and pointed, either shaped rather like forceps for extricating insects from bark crevices and picking them from vegetation, or flat and broad at the base with long bristles in the upper mandible, used to capture insects in flight.

The feet are equipped with four medium-long toes; three point forward and the thicker hind toe points backward; they show that most songbirds are adapted to an arboreal way of life. People often wonder how birds can sleep on a thin twig or similar perch without falling off. In fact the toes grasp the twig automatically; the movement of the toes is controlled by tendons connected through the heel to the calf muscle. As the bird alights on a branch, the tendons on the outer arc of the leg are stretched by the bird's weight, the pull causing the toes to grip (see Fig. 2). The grip is further enhanced by the shape of tendons on the surface of the soles: they have an uneven surface, and teeth-like projections on the sheath catch on them. The weight of the bird's body causes these 'teeth' to fit into gaps on the tendon surface, so that the tendons are stretched without any muscular exertion.

The exposed, bare leg of a songbird (the tarsus, or, more accurately, the metatarsus) has one very distinctive feature: the front is covered by scales and the rear by a continuous, smooth surface, the so-called shoe, which is keel-shaped in almost all songbirds. Only larks have the rear of the metatarsus scaled and rounded (see Fig. 3).

6

Fig. 1. Topography of the bird's body; 1 — upper mandible, 2 — forehead, 3 — crown, 4 — cheek, 5 — occipital region, 6 — nape, 7 — back, 8 — wing coverts, 9 — scapulars, 10 — rump, 11 — upper tail coverts, 12 — tail feathers, 13 — under tail coverts, 14 — primaries, 15 — toes, 16 — tarsus, 17 — belly, 18 — breast, 19 — carpal joint, 20 — crop, 21 — throat, 22 — lower mandible

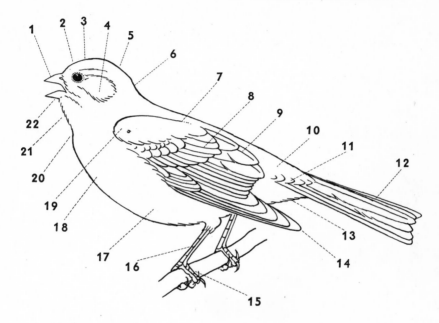

The plumage of songbirds is usually thick with the down-layer poorly developed, although the Dipper is a notable exception, its rather dense layer of down being an obvious adaptation to an aquatic way of life. Most songbirds fly well, but the shape of their tails and wings varies greatly. Generally speaking, birds with short, rounded wings tend to avoid open country and to fly for short distances (e.g. tits), while birds with longer, more pointed wings are adapted to living and flying in more open situations (e.g. flycatchers). The tail usually contains twelve feathers; the wings have ten primaries, the first usually being vestigial. The primaries are numbered from the outermost one inwards, as shown in Fig. 4.

Plumage colour is an important distinguishing feature in all birds. The coloration is caused by pigments deposited in form of microscopic particles in the barbules and barbicels of the feathers. Two basic groups of pigments are involved here: melanins, producing the black, brown and grey colours, and lipochromes, giving rise to yellow or red colours found, for example, in crossbills. It is interesting that this latter kind of coloration is highly unstable and often fades. Apart from these pigments, coloration is largely conditioned by structural coloration based on physical-optical phenomena. For instance, white coloration is caused by the air within cellular chambers. So far, blue and green have not been mentioned. If these air-filled cellular chambers are founded on a layer of dark pigments (melanins), they produce a blue tint, such as that seen in the wing-feathers of the Jay; the combination with a yellow pigment results in a green hue. The conspicuous metallic sheen in Rooks and Crows is produced by the physical structure of the feathers — by the refraction of light on the microscopic prismatic cells within a feather.

A full-grown feather is a completely horny organ, and contains no living cells. Thus it cannot change its coloration by a shift of pigments. Nevertheless, birds are known to modify their coloration without moulting: how can this happen? A change of colour can be due to abrasion or the wearing down of wing-tips. Among songbirds, the Starling is noticeably spotted and streaked in autumn, but by spring, its plumage becomes much more uniform in colour; this is caused by abrasion of the light tips of the contour feathers. Similarly, the spring colour on the Chaffinch's head is a result of the brown feather tips wearing away to reveal the blue-grey centres of the feathers.

In many passerine birds, the two sexes are differently coloured, a phenomenon known as sexual dimorphism. Males are more colourful than the females. Sexual dimorphism is linked to courtship and to the male's defence of his nesting territory against rivals of the same species.

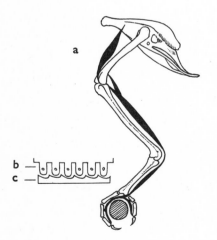

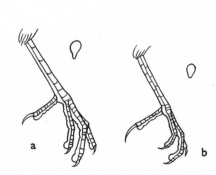

Fig. 2. a — schematic illustration of the muscle *Musculus ambiens,* b — tendon with protuberances, c — tendinous sheath with incisions

Fig. 3. Tarsus in songbirds: a — Starling (scales in front, a smooth, keel-shaped surface in back), b — Skylark (scales on both parts, the back is rounded as seen in section)

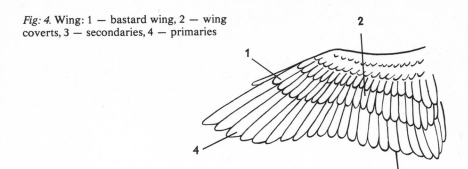

Fig: 4. Wing: 1 — bastard wing, 2 — wing coverts, 3 — secondaries, 4 — primaries

Internal features

Passerines show a number of distinctive internal features; for example, their cranial bones have a characteristic structure and they have a maximum of fifteen cervical vertebrae. The alimentary tract in seedeaters is equipped with a well-developed crop, a pouch-like enlargement of the oesophagus, in which dry and tough food stays for some time and becomes softened. Seedeaters also have a powerful, muscular stomach, lined with a thick layer of muscles and functioning as a grinding organ processing seeds softened in the crop. The grinding is facilitated by swallowed grit and stones.

The major anatomical feature of the passerines is the structure of the vocal organ or syrinx, which is similar in structure in all songbirds and helps to classify them into a common order. The syrinx is a complicated organ enabling passerine birds to sing and produce many other sounds. It may be surprising to reflect that birds such as the Raven, the Crow, the Magpie and the Jay are 'songbirds' — their unpleasant croaking and rasping can hardly be called singing! Nevertheless, they are true passerine birds as their vocal organs closely resemble those of the most accomplished songbirds.

The vocal organ is situated at the end of the trachea, at the point where the trachea branches into two bronchial tubes. It is a small drum, formed by the several tracheal and bronchial bony rings. Externally, it is connected to several pairs of tiny vocal muscles. The internal walls of the bronchial tubes unite via a cartilaginous or bony bridge which passes to a membranous vocal chord. The passage of air through the vocal organ is regulated by two vocal glottides, controlled by external and internal vocal labia and lined with drum membranes. The stretching of drum membranes by means of vocal muscles and the vibration of the membranous chord produces the sound amplified by the surrounding lung sacs (see Fig. 5).

Singing is the prerogative of males, despite the fact that the vocal organs of females hardly differ from those of their partners. Songbirds can produce a rich variety of sounds, creating a 'birds' language', in which each call has a special purpose. Many vocal expressions are closely connected to the breed-

9

ing period and are produced only (or predominantly) in this season. They include above all the song, treated in detail below. There is, however, a whole range of other calls. In gregarious species, the contact call represents the most frequent vocal display: it is a stereotyped, usually simple call, used by the birds to attract attention and contact each other. Birds utter it in a reflex manner in order to stimulate their partners to take off or alight and to be able to communicate mutually. This phenomenon is very distinct in Goldfinches or Crossbills. The alarm call is supposed to warn of danger. It is also typical in terms of species and purpose: Blackbirds and Jays are well-known for their notorious alarm calls. From their rattle, we can find out if the warning concerns an aerial predator (raptor) or a ground predator (cat, man). Birds have a call of anxiety, a call used by the young, and so on. A great number of calls can be made by one species; e.g. seven different vocal expressions have been identified in the Chaffinch; the Collared and the Pied Flycatchers have fifty common calls, out of which only two can be positively distinguished (song and alarm).

Food

Passerine birds are not categorically classified as insectivorous birds, seedeaters, berry-eaters, etc. Many insectivorous birds, e.g. warblers, feed on berries for a part of the year, mainly in late summer and in autumn. The majority of seedeaters, on the other hand, feed their young insects (e.g. Tree Sparrow), and only a few species actually bring them seeds (Goldfinch). The diet varies remarkably even in adults during the year: e.g. in the Blackbird or the Starling the animal component prevails in spring, while in summer both species concentrate gradually on fruits such as cherries, grapes or olives. Some birds are truly omnivorous, e.g. Corvines; others are strictly specialized in their food habits, e.g. Crossbills, which consume almost exclusively seeds of conifers; the adaptation to this food has become apparent in the conspicuous shape of the beak.

Some songbirds set up 'larders' for periods of food shortage: Shrikes impale their prey in thorns, the Nutcracker hides the seeds of the mountain pine or hazel nuts in various places — and is able to find its caches even under deep snow cover. The same applies to the Jay and its stores of acorns. Many stored seeds, however, remain untouched and sprout up in the germinating period: some bird species in this way contribute to the natural regeneration of trees and other plants. In connection with the distribution of seeds, it is interesting that a high percentage of them, having passed through the alimentary tract, do not lose their germinating capacity — e.g. in the Robin, it is 80 per cent, in the Song Thrush up to 85 per cent. Passerine birds also spread many poisonous plants, consuming their fruits without after-effects. Thrushes eat Belladonna seeds, Warblers feed on Daphne, etc. The Mistle Thrush and the Waxwing are noted for disseminating mistletoe — the seeds pass through the alimentary tract in seven to ten minutes. It is an extremely rapid passage,

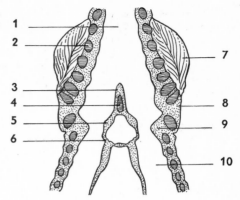

Fig. 5. Syrinx in songbirds: 1 — trachea, 2 — cartilaginous rings, 3 — glottal protuberance, 4 — pessulus, 5 — internal vocal labium, 6 — internal drum membrane, 7 — vocal muscles, 8 — external drum membrane, 9 — external vocal labium, 10 — bronchial tube

which is caused by the easy digestibility of some vegetable food, chiefly pulpy fruits. The Great Grey Shrike digests a mouse in three hours; the digestion of hard insects lasts even longer, but the maximum time is taken by tough seeds which have to stay in the crop to be softened.

Birds have the most intense metabolism known in vertebrates. The smaller a bird is, the more its body surface increases relatively. The bird accordingly loses more body warmth and requires more food. In songbirds, represented predominantly by small birds, this rule is of great importance. The daily food consumption of small insectivorous birds constitutes approximately one half of their body weight. Larger birds can survive longer without food; raptors are particularly resistant to hunger. In them, it is a biological necessity; if they do not catch any food, they have to go hungry for several days. In small insectivorous birds (tits, Goldcrests and others), an increased energy consumption in winter, followed by only a few hours of fasting, can lead to starvation and death.

Reproduction

Almost all the smaller songbirds reach sexual maturity in the year following hatching, with the exception of corvids. The majority of songbirds live in pairs, chiefly for a short term only, but rarely also throughout the year (Marsh Tits). If the birds nest several times in a year, the couple usually remain together during the whole breeding period, although a swap can take place at the second nesting attempt. Polygamy also occurs, with one male having several female partners (Pied Flycatcher).

In the majority of birds, pairs form after courtship, in which the male attempts in various ways to attract the female's attention. He can do this by ruffling his feathers, spreading his tail and wings, executing various movements or aerial acrobatics, or delivering various calls. In songbirds the song

11

plays a vital part, although it is often erroneously explained as a display meant only for the female. The song is supposed to lure her, but to a considerable extent it is an indication to neighbouring males — at the beginning of the breeding period most passerine birds settle in certain territories, selected almost entirely by males. The male sings very intensely in order to notify other males that the territory is occupied and guarded. If another male penetrates a staked-out territory, a confrontation is immediately produced between the two rivals (in spring, it can be observed in Robins, Chaffinches or Yellowhammers); the quarrel ends by one of the males being chased from the territory. The defence of a territory has probably arisen from a need to secure a sufficient quantity of food and to have security to rear young without interference. The males become quiet at the end of the nesting season, when the need to defend a territory is usually over. British Robins are one of the exceptions: they are resident and sing throughout the year. Songbirds have nesting territories with a radius of 50 to 70 metres around the nest. In birds living in colonies, e.g. Rooks, the territory is restricted to the nest itself and to the distance of a stroke of the beak.

Let us consider singing in more detail: the young inherit the capacity only partially, enriching their repertoire by listening to the adults. Songs of members of the same species are not alike; there are 'good' and 'poor' songsters, various local dialects, etc. If the young males are to acquire the best song of their species, they have to hear the most accomplished songsters. Some species lack a specific song; they imitate voices of other species (Icterine Warbler).

The nest is generally built solely by the female; the male sometimes assists her in searching for the building material (Linnet). Other males may start the construction before the female's arrival (warblers), or carry out the basic construction before their mates arrange the interior (Wren). In some songbirds the building instinct is so strong that they make several nests (Wren). Songbirds are builders of the most intricate nests, including woven domed nests and sometimes even more remarkably elaborate constructions (the Long-tailed Tit's spherical nest, the 'boxes' of Willow and Wood Warblers, the artfully hung baskets of Reed Warblers or Golden Orioles, etc.). The nests serve mainly to rear the young and are usually not used afterwards — although a few species, like tits, may continue to sleep in their nest holes.

The majority of females start incubation after completing the clutch, but corvids and Crossbills often sit from the laying of the first egg. The incubation is performed mainly by females, although the males often help in some way — they guard and feed their mates on the nest (corvids) or relieve them during incubation (Starling, House Sparrow). However, in Wrens the male takes almost no care of his partner at all.

Tits lay the highest number of eggs, sometimes as many as 12 to 15. The total number of eggs produced by songbirds is increased by the regular habit of going through two or even three nesting cycles in a single year. The size of the clutch is naturally influenced by the climate and the abundance of food. For instance, the Starling breeds twice a year in central Europe, but only once in northern Europe. It is interesting that moving from the south northwards, songbirds produce increasingly large clutches; e.g. the average clutch of the Collared Flycatcher in Hungary is 5.5 eggs, in Czechoslovakia 5.7 eggs, and in Poland 6.1 eggs.

All passerine birds are nidicolous (they feed their young); the young when they hatch are little developed, being bare or covered by scarce down, blind, deaf and scarcely mobile. They are entirely dependent on parental care; this consists mainly of feeding and keeping them warm and dry. In insectivorous songbirds the parents always feed only one chick at a time, which for several minutes afterwards does not demand any food while its siblings are fed. The seedeaters regurgitate food from the crop regularly for all the young in several subsequent doses. Young nestlings demand food with wide-open gapes, producing piping notes, which is not done by the chicks of other birds. Hygiene in the nest is handled by the parents: in the first days they swallow the droppings, but later remove them from the nest. After feeding, the young of small songbirds empty their bowels, and the parents provide a comical sight as they wait to carry the droppings off literally from the anal orifice of a nestling. The droppings are usually wrapped in a fine membrane produced in the terminal section of the intestine.

After fledging, the behaviour of parents towards their offspring differs: some chase them out from the environs (Robin), others stay with them for several months (tits), or remain in flocks with them for life (some corvids).

Population of songbirds and its regulation

One viewpoint is that the general rule of reproduction is to maintain the number of individuals of a species at a steady level. The number of the young reaching sexual maturity will approximately replace the number of adult birds which die. Small songbirds which do not migrate to winter quarters, e.g. tits or Goldcrests, are subject to considerable privations in winter, and often suffer losses of up to 80 per cent, later replaced by larger and repeated clutches. The large clutches, however, cannot in themselves secure a high production of offspring. Losses of eggs and nestlings are caused by various external factors. They are generally more marked in birds with nests situated outside holes than in hole-nesters. In the Yellowhammer, the young hatch only from 41 per cent of eggs laid; in the Collared Flycatcher the percentage is 71. According to statistical data the mortality rate of small songbirds is highest in the first year of life — mainly in nestlings. Out of 100 hatched young, only 77 Greenfinches and Robins become fledglings; other figures include 78 out of 100 Song Thrushes, 81 Spotted Flycatchers, and 88 Pied Flycatchers. When the losses of eggs are included the total loss becomes more pronounced. It can be generalized that out of all the eggs laid, approximately two-thirds are hatched by hole-nesters, and half by birds using 'open' nests (in comparison with only one-quarter in game birds). Of the fledglings, sexual maturity and first nesting are reached by 23 per cent of Robins, 20 per cent of Yellowhammers and only 13 per cent of Great Tits, which means a mortality rate in the first year of life averaging 78 to 87 per cent. Against the enormous mortality rate of the young, that of the adults is relatively low. It was found in one British population of Robins that out of 130 marked birds, 94 perished during the first year of life, 17 during the second year, 14 in the third year, 3 in the fourth year, and one in the fifth and sixth years.

Immediately following fledging, young birds are more prevalent than adults; their high mortality rate leads to a rapid increase in the proportion of adults. In following years, the composition of populations differs according to the age of the respective birds. A sample in songbirds could be provided by one population of the Pied Flycatcher, in which year-old birds formed 59 per cent and five-year-olds only 3 per cent of the nesting population. On the other hand, in birds with long life-spans, e.g. the White Stork, the year-old birds represented 17 per cent and the five-year-olds 2 per cent. Larger birds generally live longer than smaller ones. A Raven in captivity has been known to reach the age of 69 years, a Chaffinch 29 years, and warblers over twenty. In the wild, birds never survive for so long.

Classification of songbirds

The order of songbirds (Passeriformes) is divided into lower systematic units mainly according to the structure of the syrinx; scales on the metatarsus and the arrangement of the muscles on the toes are other additional criteria. These features are not as easily susceptible to modification by environmental influence as other more convenient and obvious external traits, such as the shape of the beak or body.

According to the structure of the syrinx, the order is divided into two distinct groups:
suborder Clamatores — clamatorial:
syrinx has only 2 (rarely 3) pairs of vocal muscles (tropical bird species);
suborder Oscines:
syrinx has more than 3, most frequently 5 to 7 pairs of vocal muscles. All the songbird species in this book are included in this exceptionally numerous suborder, which is itself divided into many families.

COLOUR ILLUSTRATIONS

Woodlark
Lullula arborea

Alaudidae

The Woodlark is often more likely to be heard than seen. Its superb song is considered by many to rival that of the Nightingale. Although the Woodlark often sings by day, its flute-like 'tooleeing' lasting regularly for a full minute or more, is also to be heard on clear nights. The Woodlark frequents the edges of woodland, including pine forests, sunny clearings, meadows, heaths, etc. It usually avoids denser, closed woodland and scrub with thick plant cover. In some parts of Europe Woodlarks arrive at their nesting grounds in March and April, although they can be seen as early as in February on snow-covered fields and meadows. In Britain and western Europe it is mainly resident. They nest from April to July and rear two broods. The nest is situated on the ground, generally in a sunny spot, well hidden in not too tall vegetation. It is composed of dry grasses and roots, sometimes of moss and lichen; the lining often consists of hairs. The female lays three to five whitish eggs with tiny brown and grey spots and incubates them alone for 13 to 15 days. Both parents feed the young for two weeks. At that time, the fledglings can be well distinguished by the conspicuous pattern inside the beak. The diet mainly consists of insects, but in the migratory period seeds are also eaten. In some parts of Europe Woodlarks depart for their winter quarters in the Mediterranean in September and October.

1

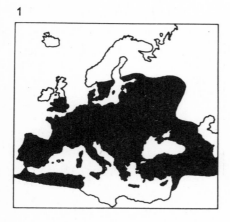

The Woodlark occurs over much of Europe, western Asia and the western part of north Africa (1). It resembles the Skylark, but it is slightly smaller, with a shorter tail, and is often more rust-coloured (2). The tail feathers are rich brown. The head is distinctive, with white eyestripes between the slightly crested crown and dark ear-coverts meeting at the nape. The sexes are similar. The songflight is very characteristic: following an almost vertical take-off, often from a treetop, the male soars and spirals above the nesting territory, with slow wing beats, and then

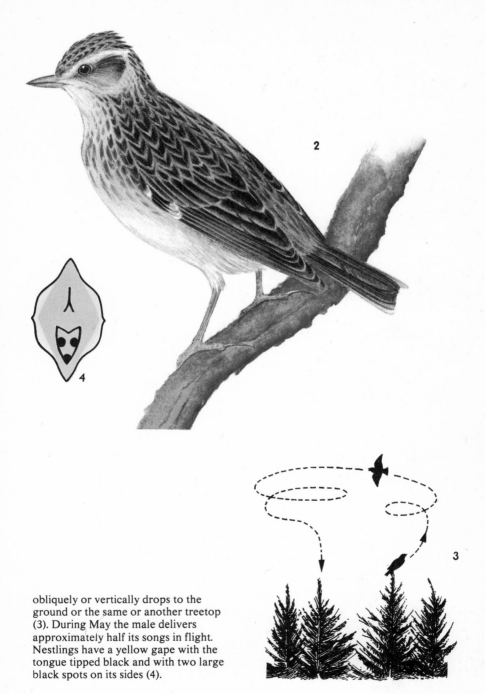

obliquely or vertically drops to the ground or the same or another treetop (3). During May the male delivers approximately half its songs in flight. Nestlings have a yellow gape with the tongue tipped black and with two large black spots on its sides (4).

Skylark
Alauda arvensis

The Skylark is distributed throughout Europe, Asia, and northern Africa. It typically inhabits woodless areas, but also lives in open cultivated and uncultivated country such as fields and lowland meadows. Skylarks are largely resident in the British Isles. The nest, woven from grass stems, thin roots and small quantities of horsehair or other hairs, is made by the female in a small hollow. She lays three to five greyish-yellow eggs with fine brownish markings, and incubates them for 12 to 14 days. The young leave the nest at 8 to 11 days of age, absolutely unable to fly; they are fed by both parents. Almost all pairs rear two broods yearly, between April and July. The food is half animal — various insects and larvae, spiders, centipedes and earthworms — and half plant material — seeds and the green parts of plants.

3

The Skylark is streaked greyish or tawny-brown above and paler below (1). The outer tail feathers are white and are very noticeable when the Skylark is flushed from the ground at short range (2). The crown feathers form a distinct crest, more prominent than that of the Woodlark. The almost straight claw of the hind toe is very distinct: it increases the supporting capacity of the foot, and facilitates movement on the ground. Females are indistinguishable from males, except their very slightly smaller size. The nestlings are characterized by their rough down; their gapes are yellow, and the tongue is marked by three black dots (3). The Skylark's song is famous and well known; it is most often delivered in flight: the male rises from the ground nearly vertically, usually to a great height; after soaring in circles he descends gradually, still singing, and finally drops abruptly to earth (4). The average length of its aerial song-flights in May is about two minutes.

2

4

1

Crested Lark
Galerida cristata

The Crested Lark is a typical resident bird in continental Europe but is very rare in Britain. It can be difficult to flush, flying only a few metres away from an approaching man. Unlike many songbirds, Crested Larks remain paired throughout the winter. In spring in central Europe, mostly in March, they leave towns for their typical sites: fallow fields and weed-covered waste grounds — garbage-dumps, building sites, railway embankments, etc. They are commonly double-brooded between April and early July. The female builds the nest from grass stems, roots and leaves (and rarely also from hairs) in a depression in the soil, assisted by the male. She alone incubates the clutch of three to five eggs (similar to those of Skylarks, but more distinctly spotted) for 12 to 13 days. The fledglings leave the nest at 9 to 10 days, although they are still unable to fly, and hide nearby. In 14 days, they are already dust-bathing in the manner of Skylarks, and they fly at the age of 20 days. Parents feed them almost exclusively on insects and worms, but the adults feed on plant food, seeds or the green parts of plants. The Crested Lark is distributed over most of Europe northward to southern Scandinavia, in central and southern Asia and in north Africa. In many places in Europe, its numbers have been diminishing recently. The Crested Lark is thought to have originated in the eastern steppes, from which it spread into Europe as agriculture expanded; it was already present in Europe in the 14th century.

The Crested Lark closely resembles the Skylark both in size and coloration (1), differing only in the shape of the crown crest (2). The female resembles the male and juveniles are more spotted and have smaller crests. The male usually sings from a vantage point on the ground, such as a lump of soil or a heap of stones, but often sings in flight too. It takes off obliquely, flying above the nesting ground with a curiously floppy action,

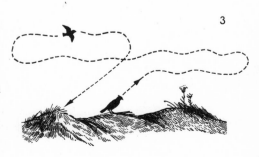

3

often to considerable distances from the nest; it rarely circles, and alights gradually, often onto some elevated point (3). The average length of its songflight is shorter than in the Skylark, generally about one minute. An interesting feature of the Crested Lark is its ability to imitate the songs of other birds.

Yellow Wagtail
Motacilla flava

Motacillidae

The Yellow Wagtail frequents damp meadows and the borders of marshes, ponds and rivers, also occurring in fields. It has a relatively short tail, and flies with a characteristic light, undulating flight. It often sits on exposed plants or bushes and calls a persistent 'tsweep'. Yellow Wagtails arrive at their nesting grounds in April, at first in small groups but later dispersing and forming pairs. Pairs occupy a relatively small nesting territory (60 metres around the nest on average) and defend it against other wagtails. In May or June, the female builds the nest, always on the ground in fairly long vegetation. It is built from the stems and leaves of grasses and roots and is lined with a thick layer of animal hair. The female lays five to six eggs, whitish and entirely covered with tiny grey-brown spots, resulting in a café-au-lait appearance. The female incubates the eggs for 13 days. The nestlings leave the nest rather early, at the age of 11 days, still unable to fly. In July some pairs rear a second brood. The Yellow Wagtail is mainly insectivorous, eating small beetles and their larvae, flies, grasshoppers, spiders, worms and small molluscs. European Wagtails prepare for migration in August and September, gathering in large flocks and roosting overnight in reed beds together with Pied or White Wagtails. They spend the winter in the Mediterranean, or as far south as central Africa; eastern races winter in southern Asia and India.

The considerable range of the Yellow Wagtail has given rise to over twenty geographical races, in which the males differ only in the pattern and coloration of the head. The females of the individual races are almost identical. The Central European Blue-headed Wagtail *(Motacilla flava flava)*, which is widespread over central Europe and central Asia, is yellow below and olive-green above with the grey-blue crown, separated from the darker line through the eye by a white stripe (1) above the eye. The female is generally paler, with a whitish throat and yellowish grey head without the stripe over the eye.

2 ♂   3 ♂   4 ♂

5 ♂

The juveniles are buff with dark spots on the throat forming an incomplete 'necklace'.

The Black-headed Wagtail *(Motacilla flava feldeggi)* has a rich black head (2); it occurs in the Balkans and in western Asia. The Grey-headed Wagtail *(M. f. thunbergi)* has a dark grey crown and dark cheeks (3); it is common in northern Europe and ranges eastwards to the Ob River. The Ashy-headed Wagtail *(M. f. cinereocapilla)* has a grey head and a white throat (4); it is confined to southern Europe, north to the Apennines. The Yellow Wagtail *(M. f. flavissima)* has a yellow-green head with a yellow stripe above the eye (5); it is restricted to Great Britain. The Spanish Wagtail *(M. f. iberiae)* of the Iberian Peninsula and southern France is an intermediate between the Blue-headed and Ashy-headed Wagtails in appearance.

1 ♂

Grey Wagtail
Motacilla cinerea

The Grey Wagtail is largely dependent on water, especially streams, and its diet consists predominantly of water insects, their larvae, and other tiny aquatic animals. In some central parts of Europe it returns to the nesting grounds in April, sometimes as early as March. Nests can be found from April onwards, usually in hollows near streams, among stones or roots on banks, in holes in various man-made constructions beside water, e.g. small bridges, dykes, walls of tow-paths; but also in walls and in the rafters of buildings situated farther from water. The nest is composed of grass stems, roots, moss and bits of leaves, and intertwined with fine plant fibres, hair and horsehair. The female lays four to six eggs. Both parents share the incubation for 12 to 14 days and together feed the chicks in the nest for another 12 to 13 days. Most pairs rear a second brood in June—July. Autumn migration takes place in September—October. Some birds in southern Europe are resident and even in central Europe, some Wagtails can be found in winter, generally near ice-free waters. The migratory populations winter in the Mediterranean and north Africa. In Britain in winter the Grey Wagtail often fills the 'niche' that the Yellow Wagtail holds in summer.

2 ♀

The Grey Wagtail might be mistaken for the Blue-headed Wagtail, but in the male the throat is black and the back is greyer; the tail is distinctly longer than in the Yellow Wagtail (1). It is altogether a more slender and elegant bird than the Yellow Wagtail. Females (2) and young birds lack the black throat patch, as does the male in winter plumage. When alighting, the male bobs the tail up and down. It flies rapidly with deep undulations, usually sounding a sharp 'tsi-sit'. The Grey Wagtail occurs over almost all of Europe (in southern Scandinavia and Denmark it appeared only at the beginning of this century), Asia and Africa (4). The eggs of the Grey Wagtail have small, dense russet spots (3) on a grey-white to greenish ground.

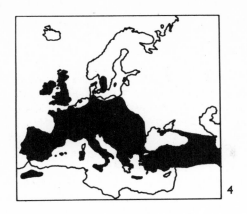

3

4

1 ♂

25

Pied or White Wagtail
Motacilla alba

Motacillidae

The Pied or White Wagtail is a widely distributed bird. It is often found near water, but it is also common far from it, in fields and pastures, quarries, isolated farms and extensive human settlements. It occurs in both lowlands and at high altitudes in mountains. It occurs all over Europe, Asia and north Africa. White Wagtails undertake their return passage from winter quarters in the Mediterranean and down to equatorial Africa in March. They immediately stake out their nesting territories, and protect them vigorously. They rear two to three broods a year, from April to August. Both adults build a cone-shaped nest of stems, roots, leaves, and pieces of moss; they line the interior with hair, horsehair, or sometimes feathers. The nest has various locations: hollows and crevices in buildings, rocks and hollow trees, but also wood piles and rafters in buildings, or simply on the ground. The colour of the eggs is whitish, powder-blue or greyish, with dark grey to brown spots; they are incubated solely by the female for a period of 12 to 14 days. During the following two weeks, the nestlings are fed by both parents. The gape of the nestling is orange-coloured with yellow edges. In August, White Wagtails gather in smallish flocks, settling in early evenings in reed beds to spend the night together with Swallows, House Martins, Starlings and other wagtails. They set out on their autumn migratory flights from September to November. Some individual birds winter in central Europe near ice-free waters. The British race, *Motacilla alba yarrellii*, is a resident in Britain or is sometimes partially migratory.

3 ♂

The Pied or White Wagtail is
a universally known bird with contrasting
black-and-white coloration. The back of
the crown, the nape, the throat, the breast
and the tail are black; the back is grey,
and other parts are white or grey (1). In
females, parts of the black coloration are
replaced by dark grey; young birds are
predominantly grey-brown with a darker
throat patch. After the summer moult,
both sexes lose the black on the chin and
throat (2); it remains only on the breast.
The huge area of Europe and Asia is
inhabited by several races, differing in the
extent of the black and grey coloration.

Great Britain and parts of extreme
western Europe inhabited by the Pied
Wagtail *(Motacilla alba yarrellii)* (3), in
which the male has a black back and
females are darker than White Wagtails.
Wagtails fly in long undulations; a few
wingbeats carry the bird up and it then
glides down with the wings closed; they
produce a two-syllable note 'tsillip-tsillip'.
When walking or at rest, they frequently
and conspicuously 'wag' their tails up and
down.

2 ♂

1 ♂

Meadow Pipit
Anthus pratensis

Motacillidae

Grassy slopes, heaths, mountains and damp lowland meadows are inhabited by a slender bird that is rather reminiscent of a small streaked Skylark — the Meadow Pipit. When it is flushed it flies up with a sharp alarm note 'tsee-tseep' (especially noticeable when a small flock is disturbed), and circles around overhead. The Meadow Pipit occurs over almost all of the northern half of Europe and western Siberia; in southern Europe it is restricted to several isolated spots. In central Europe it is a migratory bird, wintering chiefly in the Mediterranean, although the northern birds sometimes stay in western and central Europe in winter, mainly around iceless waters. In March and May, small flocks fly to their nesting grounds, returning to the winter quarters in September to November. In western Europe and the British Isles the migratory pattern of the populations is complex with some birds migrating south, while others remain behind and are joined by immigrants from further north. The nest, woven from dry grass or moss and lightly lined with hairs, is well hidden in the grass. In April or May the female lays four to six greyish, brown-spotted eggs, and incubates them for about 13 days. Some pairs produce a second brood in June and early July. Nestlings are nursed by both parents; they stay in the nest for 12 to 14 days before fledging. At first they are unable to fly, and hide in the long vegetation. The nesting territory is relatively small, reaching approximately 100 metres from the nest. The Meadow Pipit feeds, like other pipits, on smaller beetles, hymenopterous insects, spiders, etc. It occasionally also feeds on seeds.

4

It is rather difficult to distinguish the
Meadow Pipit from the Tree Pipit by
plumage alone, but the Meadow Pipit
tends to have a darker back, and the
breast is more white. The female and
male are identical (1). Under the tail
coverts it may be spotted (2); the second

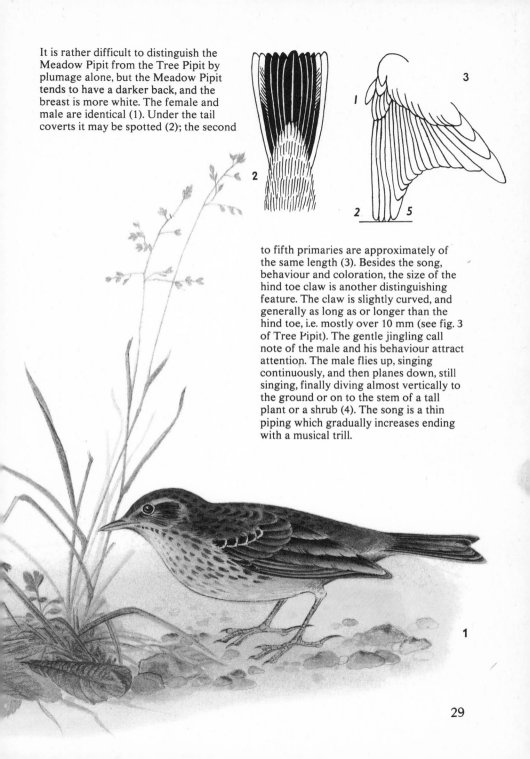

to fifth primaries are approximately of
the same length (3). Besides the song,
behaviour and coloration, the size of the
hind toe claw is another distinguishing
feature. The claw is slightly curved, and
generally as long as or longer than the
hind toe, i.e. mostly over 10 mm (see fig. 3
of Tree Pipit). The gentle jingling call
note of the male and his behaviour attract
attention. The male flies up, singing
continuously, and then planes down, still
singing, finally diving almost vertically to
the ground or on to the stem of a tall
plant or a shrub (4). The song is a thin
piping which gradually increases ending
with a musical trill.

Tree Pipit
Anthus trivialis

Motacillidae

The song of one of our best songsters, the Tree Pipit, can be heard most often in clearings or margins of deciduous and coniferous forests in both mountains and lowlands, on overgrown hill slopes and also in damp meadows with thinly scattered trees. The middle part of its song resembles that of the canary and for this reason it is sometimes called the 'forest canary'. Tree Pipits spend a great deal of time on the ground, walking to and fro, flicking their tails and hindquarters. When disturbed they usually seek refuge on trees and sound an alarm note resembling 'seep-seep'. They run lengthwise along tree branches. The Tree Pipit is found throughout much of Europe, eastwards to Siberia and central Asia. It leaves its winter quarters in the Mediterranean and in Africa early in April, appearing at first in fields and meadows and then starting to sing on the nesting grounds, usually in mid-April or in May. The female weaves the nest of grass stalks, leaves and lichens, sometimes lining it with fur, situating it on the ground under a tuft of grass. She lays five to six eggs, remarkably variable in colour, from powder-blue to brown-pink, with small and larger dark spots; she alone incubates them for 12 to 13 days. The same time is devoted by the parent birds to feeding the young. Some pairs rear a second brood, generally in June or July. Families of Tree Pipits leave the breeding area during September—October.

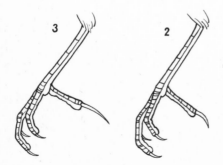

The Tree Pipit is Skylark-coloured, olive-brown above with dark longitudinal stripes, and has a pale brown breast with pronounced dark brown streaks (1). Both sexes are identically coloured. The important fact for determination of a specimen in the hand is the claw of the hind toe, which is shorter than the toe (by about 3 mm) and is strongly curved (2).

The difference can be observed in Fig. 3 which shows the toe of the Meadow Pipit. The male sings mainly in flight. It takes to the air from a tree top, flying obliquely up, starts to sing, and descends in an arc, with spread wings and tail, to the same or other tree top, finishing its song with a distinct and characteristic 'seea-seea-seea' (4). Nests of Tree Pipits are often chosen by Cuckoos for their parasitic egg-laying.

Tawny Pipit
Anthus campestris

Motacillidae

The Tawny Pipit is aboriginal to the steppes of eastern Europe, but in addition to steppe areas it can be encountered on dry, stone-strewn slopes, bare fallows, dry sunny glades, and large fields. It generally favours warm areas. The nest of dry grass, roots, sometimes of bits of moss and a small quantity of hairs in the lining is built in a depression in the ground. It is covered on top by grass, heather, etc. The eggs are highly variable, being less spotted than in the other pipits, so that the ground colour of greyish, brownish or greenish can be seen. The clutch of four to five eggs is incubated by the female for 13 to 14 days. The male does not share the incubation, although he assists in the feeding of the young. In about 14 days, the nestlings are fledged enough to leave the nest. Parents continue looking after them for some more time in the area near the nest until they are independent. Some pairs rear a second brood; the nesting season extends from May to July. The nesting territory is extensive, on average 200 to 300 metres around the nest site. At the end of August and during September the Tawny Pipits leave their nesting grounds.

3

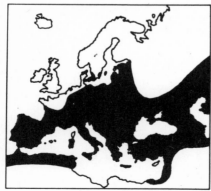

The Tawny Pipit differs from all other pipits by its almost uniform, sandy-brown back, and by its almost unspotted underparts (1). The male and female are identical. This coloration produces an overall light-coloured impression. The Tawny Pipit is the largest of all the pipits described; it is a slender bird, with a rather long tail and pale-coloured legs. It moves almost exclusively on the ground and flies in deep undulations (2).

2

It can be recognized by its voice: its call sounds like 'zirluih-zirluih', which is not unlike the song delivered by the male as he flies in wide circles, usually far from the nest. The Tawny Pipit is resident in central and southern Europe, north Africa, and the temperate zone of Asia. In winter it flies to north and central Africa and to southern Asia, returning to its breeding grounds in April and May (3).

1

Red-throated Pipit

Anthus cervinus

Motacillidae

The Red-throated Pipit is found in the far north of Europe and Asia, chiefly inhabiting the northern marshes and tundra. It prefers damp, grassy areas covered by stunted birches and willows, but is also found in meadows with groups of shrubs in the vicinity of Lapp houses and farms. It often sits on bushes, fences, electric wires, etc. Due to northern climatic conditions, breeding is delayed until June and July, and consequently its migration through central Europe can be observed only in the late spring, usually in May. It rears only one brood a year. The female conceals the nest under grass or stunted shrubs; it is built with grass stalks and moss, lined with softer grass and occasionally with hairs. She hatches four to six eggs, similar to those of the Meadow Pipit, but with larger and darker spots. The female incubates them for approximately 13 days, and after a similar period the young leave the nest. From that time, the male helps to feed them. In September and October Red-throated Pipits migrate from their northern nesting grounds far to the south, to east Africa and southern Asia. They can be observed individually and in flocks in central and southern Europe, most frequently on banks of ponds and rivers, or in meadows.

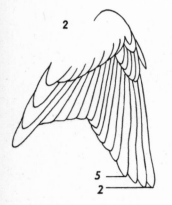

The Red-throated Pipit in autumn and winter largely resembles the Meadow Pipit but has a more prominently spotted pattern above, and bold, black-spotted under tail coverts (1). The second to fifth primaries towards the inside of the wing become distinctly shorter (2). It is the only pipit manifesting noticeable sexual dimorphism: the male in his nuptial dress (3) is distinguished from the female by the cinnamon-red throat.

In a flock of migrating Meadow Pipits, the Red-throated Pipit can be recognized by its call. When taking to the air, it produces a two-syllabled 'dee-er-er' or a shrill 'see-er', similarly to the Reed Bunting.

3 ♂

Lesser Grey Shrike

Lanius minor

Laniidae

The Lesser Grey Shrike frequents open country dotted with taller trees, or groups of trees, tree-lined roads, field margins, orchards and forest borders. It prefers deciduous trees and only occasionally occurs among conifers. It regularly chooses tall trees for nesting; often poplars. The nest is frequently found above 10 metres from the ground, usually near the trunk or at the base of a large bough. The nest is rather large, made of twigs, roots and thick grass stalks, softly lined with feathers, plant wool and hairs. A feature characteristic of the nest of the Lesser Grey Shrike is the large and conspicuous quantity of green plants woven into the middle section of the nest. In May or June, the female lays four to six greenish eggs covered by tiny dark spots, and sits on them for about 15 days. The nestlings are fed by both parents for roughly two weeks in the nest, and for a longer period after they fledge. The diet is exclusively animal, as in the Red-backed Shrike. Unlike other shrikes the Lesser Grey Shrike rarely impales its prey on thorns. Shrikes have stout bills; the upper bill is hooked at the tip, provided with a notch — a sharp 'tooth' — enabling the bird to crush the chitinous armour of insects and to hold the hard and slippery prey. This quality is common to all shrikes.

4

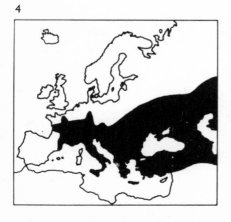

The Lesser Grey Shrike can easily be mistaken for the Great Grey Shrike. It differs in several ways: it is markedly smaller, has a broad black band over the forehead and eyes, and the breast is pale and often pink-tinged (1, 2). When determining a specimen in hand, it is important to know that the first primary is of the same length as the wing coverts, not surpassing the white area of the wing. The second, third and fourth primaries (3) are the longest flight feathers. The female largely resembles the male, but the underparts are less pinkish. In young birds, the black is replaced by brown-black, the grey-brown back and flanks are barred and the forehead is not black. It is found from southern France through southern and central Europe to Asia, as far as the Yenisei River (4). The winter quarters are in Africa, chiefly south of the equator. The Lesser Grey Shrike returns to its nesting grounds in May and leaves in late August.

1 ♂

2

Red-backed Shrike

Lanius collurio

Laniidae

The Red-backed Shrike is a typical migratory bird, spending only 4 to 5 months on its nesting grounds. It arrives in May and leaves in late August and September. Its range covers a large part of Europe from the northern borders of the Pyrenees to central Scandinavia, and a vast section of Asia. It has become increasingly rare in the western parts of its range. Its winter quarters are very extensive: European birds fly to tropical and south Africa, Asiatic birds also to India and eastern Asia (4). The Red-backed Shrike frequents open, dry country with extensive scrub, forest margins, orchards, gardens and clearings in woods, but may also be found in fields with perhaps a single bush. Its nest is usually situated low above the ground, most frequently at a height of 1 to 3 metres, often in thorny bushes. The nest is a rather massive construction built of roots and dry stalks, sometimes with bits of moss, and is lined with delicate roots and grasses, or more rarely with feathers and hairs. It is built by both adult birds. The four to six eggs are grey-green or brownish with brown spots forming a rough circle around the larger end; the female alone incubates them for 14 to 16 days. The rearing of the young in the nest takes roughly the same time, and the parents tend the fledged young for another three weeks. They rear only one brood during a year. The young are covered by down, while their skin is almost orange-coloured, and the gape of a nestling is ochre-yellow with lighter edges. Cuckoos often lay their eggs in nests of Red-backed Shrikes. The mainstay of the Red-backed Shrike's food is insects, and more rarely small vertebrates such as voles, mice, and small songbirds.

2 ♂

The pale grey head and neck, pale underparts, russet back, and black band over the eyes and forehead give the male Red-backed Shrike a beautiful appearance (1, 2). The female is rust-brown above and off-white below with darker barring (3) on the breast and flanks. Young birds resemble the female, but are also barred on the back. Shrikes have relatively long tails, which they often flick up and down — faster when they are agitated. The impaling of prey on thorns is a characteristic feature. The

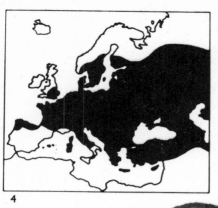

territory is not too large, generally 100 metres around the nest. Although the male spends little time at his song-posts, his vocal repertoire is very extensive; and he is a good mimic of other birds.

3 ♀

1 ♂

Woodchat Shrike
Lanius senator

The Woodchat Shrike is a bird of the warmer, sunnier regions of Europe. It prefers sunny southern slopes with thinly scattered trees or bushes, where it can be found along the margins of field groves, along roads, or in orchards. It arrives at its favourite nesting sites in late April or in May. Soon after arrival it begins to build the nest in bushes or in trees — often fruit trees. The nest is made of dry stalks and roots, decorated mainly on the edges by green plants, as in the case of the Lesser Grey Shrike. The lining comprises a thick layer of hairs, feathers and plant wool, not dry plants and rootlets as in the Red-backed Shrike. The female lays four to six eggs, resembling those of the Red-backed Shrike in size and colour, and sits on them for 14 to 15 days. The male brings her food during the whole incubation period. The young leave the nest after 19 to 20 days; the parents feed them for another 2 to 3 weeks. Each pair rears only one brood in a season. At the end of August and early in September, Woodchat Shrikes leave for their winter quarters in tropical Africa and the southern part of Arabia.

3

The Woodchat Shrike is slightly larger than the Red-backed Shrike, and is perhaps the most colourful of all shrikes (1). The russet colour of the nape and neck contrasts sharply with the black mask extending over the forehead and eyes; the black wings show large white patches, and the tail is black, edged with white. The underparts and rump are creamy white. The female closely resembles the male, but is paler. The young are reddish-grey above and paler below, with rich brown barring on the upper and underparts. They have a pronounced, large clear spot on the

2

1 ♂

shoulders and a smaller one at the base of primaries — the first indication of future white wing-markings. The Woodchat Shrike is particularly striking when seen in flight (2). The Woodchat inhabits southern, western and central Europe, the Mediterranean islands, north-western Africa and western Asia (3).

41

Great Grey Shrike
Lanius excubitor

Laniidae

The Great Grey Shrike has an almost world-wide distribution. It is found in parts of every continent except Australia, and over almost all of Europe (excluding the British Isles, where it is a scarce winter visitor only), the Apennines and the Balkan Peninsula, Asia, northern Africa and northern parts of North America. This vast distribution has naturally given rise to many geographical races. Unlike other shrikes, the Great Grey Shrike is predominantly a resident bird. Only birds living in the northernmost areas affected by severe frosts leave in winter for more southerly regions. At that time, they can be usually encountered in fields and meadows, sitting for long periods on tree-tops which serve as look-out posts as they search for their main prey — small rodents. At times of food shortage, 'caches' or 'larders' of the Great Grey Shrike can be found: these consist of voles impaled on thorns — either whole animals or parts of them — and also insects, occasional lizards and small songbirds. The prey is not always im-paled; it is sometimes stuck in the fork of a branch. The Great Grey Shrike lives predominantly in open country with groups of trees, in clearings in woods and along forest margins. From April to June its large nest of dry twigs, roots and stalks, lined with plant wool, hairs or feathers, is in use. The female incubates the clutch of five to seven greenish, brown-spotted eggs for 15 to 16 days. The rearing of nest-lings takes about 20 days, but both parents feed their offspring for two weeks outside the nest. The territory of the Great Grey Shrike may be extensive, embracing a radius of 1 kilometre from the nest.

The Great Grey Shrike is the largest of all shrikes. Both sexes are similarly coloured (1): the grey back and whitish underparts are complemented by black wings, black tail with white edges, and a black eye-patch. There is usually a double white wing-bar on the primaries and secondaries, but individual specimens with a single bar only also exist, reminiscent of the Lesser Grey Shrike. The basic distinctive mark is the black mask, extending to the bill but not to the forehead. The first primary is about half the size of the second one surpassing the white area of the wing; the third, fourth and fifth primaries are the longest (2).

The second primary is shorter than the fifth. Young birds have fawn-grey backs, and the breast and flanks are barred crosswise (3). The Great Grey Shrike typically flies in long undulations, but it can also hover in one spot when searching for prey.

Waxwing
Bombycilla garrulus

Bombycillidae

The Waxwing inhabits coniferous and mixed forests of the northern type, i.e. taigas and tundras. It is single-brooded, habitually nesting in June. The nest is built of tiny twigs, moss, lichens and grass, lined with feathers and hairs, and situated in a tree. The four to six bluish eggs, sparsely covered by brown and black spots, are incubated by the female alone for approximately 14 days. The male brings food to his mate, and both then take care of the young, which leave the nest after 14 to 16 days. At that time Waxwings and their young feed on insects, mostly mosquitoes, which are abundant in taigas and tundras. Later they move on to plant matter, searching for berries which they consume in large quantities. Their digestion is extremely rapid: the food passes straight through the stomach and intestines and is often only half-digested when it leaves the alimentary tract. Waxwings in this way help to distribute the seeds of many trees and shrubs. In more southerly areas Waxwings can usually be found only in winter, roughly from October or November to March, when they wander around looking for food. They are remarkably tame, taking no notice of people. In some years their arrival takes the form of an enormous invasion, caused probably by an extreme increase in their numbers combined with a shortage of food in the north. Following such an invasion, only a small number returns to the north.

2

The Waxwing is one of the most attractive birds. Its rich, soft plumage of predominantly grey-brown colour with a reddish tinge contrasts with the bold patterns of black chin and eye-band, black primaries with bright yellow tips, and black, yellow-tipped tail. There are two large white spots in the wings and the secondaries are tipped with waxy, red, horny blobs, most noticeable in adult

1

3

males. The area under the tail is a deep red. The alluring appearance is further enhanced by a conspicuous crest (1). The female closely resembles the male; the chin and throat in young birds are not black but off-white. The breeding range of the Waxwing is the northernmost parts of Europe, Asia, and North America (2) (which is inhabited by a small *Bombycilla cedrorum* [3]).

Swallow
Hirundo rustica

The Swallow is one of the most accomplished masters of flying; it is airborne for the greater part of the day and must fly many kilometres between dawn and dusk. The air is also the environment providing its food — flying insects. The wide gape, extending behind the eyes, helps the Swallow to catch them. It is unable to obtain much other food, and as a result Swallows sometimes starve to death if especially cold weather occurs during migration. Chilly and rainy summers also cause shortages in insects and cause the hungry Swallows to spend more time feeding over water surfaces where insects are more abundant. The first Swallows in spring are likely to be seen near water. When nesting, the Swallow actually seeks the presence of man: its nest is most often found within human settlements, in cowsheds, porches, garages, stables, passages or even in rooms, and less frequently on exterior walls. Early in May the Swallow lays four to six white, russet-spotted eggs, which are incubated by the female alone for 14 to 16 days. The male provides her with food, and both rear the hatched chicks. For three weeks, and then for several days after fledging, they bring them insects and feed them. They then start preparing their next clutch, usually laid in the same nest. Sometimes they start a third brood, but the young of this clutch do not always manage to mature sufficiently before the migratory flight and may not survive. After the nesting period Swallows gather in large flocks, often comprising thousands of birds, and often roost in vast numbers in reedbeds prior to their departure southwards in September and October. The Swallow is found over a vast part of the world: Europe, Asia, north Africa, and almost the whole of North America. European Swallows winter in equatorial and southern Africa, those from the Asiatic area from India to the Philippines; the North American ones leave for northern parts of South America. European Swallows return to their home countries in late March and April.

The Swallow is a slender, elegant, blue-black bird with a russet forehead (1) and throat and creamy-white underparts. In flight it can be best distinguished from the similar House Martin by its long, slender tail-streamers (2) and its all-dark upperparts. The young are duller in colour, with the throat patch less

pronounced and the outer tail-feathers much shorter (3). The nest is saucer-shaped, open above, and the birds build it from pieces of mud mixed with saliva (4). They often bring the mud in their tiny beaks from far away and stick the bits together like bricks, strengthening them with stalks of grass or straw; these sometimes hang down from the nest, making it look untidy. The relatively deep interior of the nest is softly lined with stalks, feathers and hairs.

47

House Martin
Delichon urbica

The House Martin is also fond of settling in the vicinity of man, although its original nesting habitat, like that of the Swallow, was rock faces and cliffs. Unlike Swallows, House Martins do not construct their nests inside buildings but on the outside walls, close to eaves, cornices or window recesses. Both partners are efficient 'bricklayers', and their nest, lacking the plant material, is more trim than the Swallow's. The parents share in the incubation of the four to six white eggs for a period of 14 to 16 days. After 20 to 23 days of being fed insects, the young are fully fledged and leave the nest as skilful fliers. During the summer, pairs of Martins usually rear two broods in one nest, and unless the nest becomes dilapidated it is repaired and used for years. House Martins tend even more than Swallows to nest in colonies; very often several nests can be stuck close to each other, under a window ledge, sometimes even piled up several storeys high. Before migration, Martins gather into flocks, sit for several days on electric wires, and then set off for their long journey to warmer climates far to the south. European House Martins winter in northern parts of Africa, leaving Europe generally in September and returning in April—May. The House Martin is native to Europe, Asia and north Africa; it is more abundant than the Swallow in mountains, breeding even in mountain chalets situated at high altitudes. It is also an excellent flier, spending many hours in the air every day, descending to the ground only to pick up building material. It walks very clumsily, with tiny steps, for its legs and feet serve merely for sitting or hanging on walls or nests. Unlike the Swallow, the Martin's feet are covered by short white feathers reaching right down to the claws.

Many people mistake the House Martin for its relative the Swallow, and vice versa, although it is not difficult to distinguish the two. The House Martin is somewhat smaller and stockier; the back is metallic blue-black in colour, and the underparts are pure white (1). In flight, it can be recognized easily by the shallow fork in the tail (2), and the conspicuous white rump (3). Both adults are identical, but the young are duller above and

2

4

3

1

whitish below with a brownish tinge. The
basic identification feature of a Martin's
nest is its shape: it is round and
completely closed, with a small oval
entrance at the top. The construction
takes approximately a week and in the
final phase it is softly lined with a heap of
feathers, hairs and grasses, which never
protrude from the entrance hole (4). If
they do, it is usually a sign that the nest
has been taken over by a Sparrow.

Sand Martin
Riparia riparia

The Sand Martin inhabits a large part of the northern hemisphere; its distribution corresponds closely to that of the Swallow. It lives in Eurasia, parts of Africa and in North America; its winter quarters are in more or less the same locations as those of the Swallow. European Sand Martins return to their respective countries at about the same time as Swallows and House Martins, but unlike them they do not seek the presence of man, nesting in a very different and extremely interesting way. They prefer vertical sand or clay walls of gravel-pits, steep river banks, or brick factories, into which they dig their nesting holes with beaks and feet. Both partners undertake the digging very energetically and the burrow is often finished in three to four days. In May the first clean white eggs appear in the nesting chambers; when the clutch reaches five to seven the parents share the incubation for 12 to 15 days. A second brood is generally reared in July. Parents feed their offspring on small insects caught in the air. At first they bring the food to the nesting chamber, but later the nestlings crawl to the entrance, sticking out their heads and loudly demanding food. They leave the secure burrow in about 3 weeks, but they return to it for a long time to roost. Throughout August and September, Sand Martins leave the colonies, which are deserted by October.

2

The Sand Martin is a comparatively inconspicuous brownish bird, rather like a small House Martin in general shape (1). Both sexes have a brown back, dirty white underparts, and a brown band (2) across the upper breast. The young differ from the adults in that the brown feathers of their upper parts have yellowish edges, which can be seen clearly only in the hand. Like all the birds of the family Hirundinidae, Sand Martins are master fliers. They nest in colonies of dozens to hundreds of pairs; nesting by solitary pairs is rare. Nesting in holes in banks brings certain disadvantages: crumbling banks undermined by water devastate many colonies; others are destroyed during the extraction of clay or sand in brick factories and gravel-pits. The nesting holes are approximately 1 m deep (50 to 150 cm) and are enlarged at the end into a smallish ball-shaped chamber lined with dry grass and lots of feathers (3).

1

3

Dipper
Cinclus cinclus

Cinclidae

If we see an active black-brown bird with a bold white gorget and a short, cocked tail near a rocky, fast-flowing stream, we know for sure that it is the Dipper, a passerine bird with a unique ability to feed in and under the water. The Dipper hunts for its food, consisting mainly of insects and their larvae, crustaceans and tiny fish, on the bottoms of streams. It demonstrates its dexterity by gripping the stones with its claws, using its wings as paddles while underwater, and not simply picking up the prey but searching for it by turning pebbles. When it emerges, it is completely dry — water slips off its perfectly waterproof feathers. The building material for the nest — mostly aquatic plants — is also gathered underwater, and sometimes on the shore, but it is immediately soaked as well. The nest is built by both partners in hollows under tree roots, in rocky crevices or under small bridges, usually in the close vicinity of water and sometimes even behind waterfalls. It is large and dome-shaped, with a side entrance. The clutch of four to six white eggs is incubated by both parents for 15 to 17 days; the young leave the nest in 3 weeks. The majority of pairs rear two broods a year, the first in April and the second in June. Despite the fact that the Dipper is a typical inhabitant of rapid streams, it is not strictly a mountain species. It is often found at lower altitudes where suitable rivers and streams occur.

3

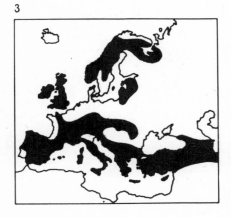

The Dipper is the size of a Thrush, but looks more like a huge Wren (1) with its rotund shape and short tail. The thick plumage is always well greased by oil secreted from the preen gland: it is impermeable and holds the air, so that a Dipper feeding underwater is encased in a protective coating of air bubbles. The plumage is basically dark brown to black, with a white throat (2) and breast. The chicks are slate-grey above and paler below with the whole plumage transversely vermiculated with darker markings. A pair occupies a large linear

52

territory, approximately one kilometre of a stream, and defends it energetically. Dippers are resident birds, wandering a little only in winter. The Dipper occurs almost all over Europe, Asia and north-western Africa (3). Its distribution in Asia is discontinuous, divided into smaller, isolated areas, which gave rise to many races.

Mountainous streams in western regions of North America are inhabited by the American Dipper *(Cinclus mexicanus),* a slate-coloured Dipper with a white circle around the eye (4).

4

1

2

Wren
Troglodytes troglodytes

Troglodytidae

This tiny, brown bird with its short, cocked tail, is extremely agile and restless, and cannot be mistaken for any other European passerine. Its favourite haunts are in clearings of various types of forests, gardens and banks of brooks lined with thick brushwood, and so on — it simply looks for thick bushes in which to hide or build its nests. It nests in low spruces, roots of dead trees or under overhanging banks. The family life of the Wren has several interesting traits. The male stakes out the nesting territory, and carries out the construction of the nest alone, building with moss, grasses and leaves. He does not make a single nest, but starts several of them. He brings in the female, attracting her by singing, and she inspects all the nests, choosing the best one. The female then lines the nest with hairs and feathers, and lays five to seven white, delicately red-spotted eggs in April or May. She incubates them alone for 14 to 16 days. The chicks leave the nest at 15 to 17 days. In June or July a second clutch is laid and then another surprising feature emerges: the young from the first brood help to look after their junior siblings, helping the parents to feed them, mostly on insects. The other nests built by the male are not wasted: these so-called 'cock's nests' are often used by the male and later by the fledglings for their sleeping quarters. Wrens remain in their nesting territories throughout winter, occasionally wandering further afield. They never fly long distances and generally move close to the ground. The Wren's song is exceptionally loud for such a tiny bird; it is probably the only songbird heard quite commonly in winter. Wrens often rear young Cuckoos in their nests.

4

The Wren is one of the smallest European birds, weighing only about 9 g. Both sexes have identical coloration: thick russet-brown plumage with rich brown streaks (1), mainly above. The young resemble the adults, but they are darker on the abdomen, and at first have distinctly shorter tails. The nest is rather large for such a minute bird; it is dome-shaped, with a side entrance (2). The Wren is found over the whole of the northern hemisphere — Europe, Asia, North America and north Africa (3).

The other Wren species live in North America. One of them, the House Wren *(Troglodytes aedon)* is fairly similar to the Wren; it has a slightly longer tail than its European counterpart (4).

Dunnock or Hedge Sparrow
Prunella modularis

Prunellidae

The Dunnock is an unobtrusive but familiar bird. It occurs in a wide variety of habitats, from coniferous forests to parks, gardens, cemeteries, hedgerows, mountainous timber, and lowland deciduous woods. It is mostly associated with low, thick vegetation. The female lays four to six eggs; she incubates them, mainly alone, for a period of 12 to 14 days. The male sometimes shares incubation duties with her. The young leave the nest in another two weeks. The Dunnock breeds twice a year, from April to July. Dunnocks from central and northern Europe are mostly migratory, wintering in western or southern Europe, but those of the lowlands, like those in Britain and elsewhere in western Europe, are sedentary. The Dunnock's diet includes both animal and plant matter. Throughout the nesting period it concentrates on insects, their larvae and pupae, and on spiders; in winter the diet includes small seeds and berries. The Dunnock moves mostly on the ground, but in spring the male sings from exposed perches in trees and bushes.

Both sexes have a blue-grey head, breast and throat; the top of the head, back and wings are rich brown, with dark spots and streaks (1). The tail feathers are uniformly coloured — unlike those of the Alpine Accentor *(Prunella collaris)* in which they are terminated by large white or ochre spots. The young resemble the adults but have dark streaks below. Dunnocks have a thin awl-like beak, wider at the base. The Dunnock inhabits most of Europe (but is absent from southern Spain, Italy and Greece), Asia Minor and the Caucasus (2). It is a migratory bird in parts of Europe returning to its native country in

3

4

March—April, but elsewhere — including Britain — it is mainly resident. Its nest, woven almost exclusively of moss and lined with hairs and moss (3) is carefully hidden in the most dense undergrowth, very often in low trees, hedges and bushes. The eggs have a distinct green-blue colour, lacking any spots (4).

Alpine Accentor
Prunella collaris

Prunellidae

The Alpine Accentor is a typical mountain songbird, confined to areas above the tree-line, nesting most frequently in high rocky sites. The nest is always perfectly concealed in rocky crevices or stone-strewn slopes, or less often under boulders and bushes on high mountainous meadows; it is particularly difficult to find. Accentors' nests have been discovered several times in the retaining walls of mountain chalets. The nest is extremely flimsy and often falls apart if taken out of the crevice. The outer side is made of dry grass stalks, the middle layer of moss, and the lining of dry grass, roots and hairs. The nesting season is extensive, from mid-May to July; some pairs breed twice a year. The clutch consists of three to five spotless eggs, incubated by both parents for about 15 days. The parents at first feed the nestlings food that has been predigested in their crop, but later bring insects or tiny invertebrates. The fledglings leave the nest at the age of 14 to 16 days. It is interesting to note that fewer fledglings are usually observed than would correspond to the size of the clutch — most often 1 to 3 young can be seen. The diet later also includes seeds of grasses and other plants; when cold weather sets in, Accentors gather near mountain chalets and obtain additional food from garbage heaps; in times of deep snow cover, they descend to lower areas and winter in places not too distant from their nesting territories. They are therefore only partial migrants, leaving the higher areas in October and November and returning in April.

2

The Alpine Accentor is the size of a Lark. The upper parts are streaked grey-brown, the underparts are grey-brown with rusty streaks on the flanks. The head, neck and breast are grey, with a conspicuous, sharply delineated white throat-patch marked with fine black stripes (1). The sexes are identical; juvenile birds have a grey, unstreaked throat, and the remaining underparts are buffish with

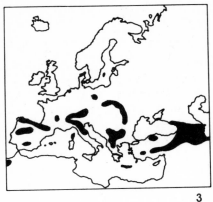

dense brown streaks. The eggs have a bright blue-green colour (2). The song of the Alpine Accentor is reminiscent of that of a Lark; the male usually sings from the ground. It is a confiding and tame bird, which can be approached to the distance of a few paces. This is probably an attribute of birds resident in places which were recently uninhabited by people. The Alpine Accentor lives in the high mountains of central and southern Europe and north Africa and right across to Japan. Its distribution is discontinuous, since the Accentor is confined to mountain ranges (3).

3

1

River Warbler
Locustella fluviatilis

Sylviidae

The River Warbler is one of those birds we hear rather than see. It lives a very secretive life in the thickest brushwoods around brooks and rivers, in the thick undergrowth of lowland woods and in wet meadows covered by dense vegetation. When disturbed, it does not generally fly away but creeps into the thickest tangle of plants, moving about with the utmost dexterity, and reminding us by its movement of a mouse rather than a bird. The nesting territory of the River Warbler is not too large, only about 50 metres around the nest. The male produces an intense song from the topmost sprigs of a bush, not only in the daytime, but quite regularly at night as well. He usually sings only until incubation and rarely after that. Its twittering song sounds like a constant repetition of 'dzee-dzee-dzee...', it is not unlike the sound of fast sawing. The song is never as long as the Grasshopper Warbler's, and the tempo is considerably slower. It arrives at its nesting grounds in late April and May. The nest of dry grasses, tree-leaves and moss is built close above the ground, often near bushes, and is lined with soft grass and sometimes hairs. The eggs are whitish, thickly spotted with russet (4). The female lays four to five eggs and sits on them for about 13 days. Both parents feed the chicks on insects and other invertebrates for approximately two weeks in the nest and for a further two weeks after fledging. They rear only one brood in a season, leaving at the end of August and in September. They are long distance travellers: their winter quarters are on the eastern coast of South Africa. The River Warbler is chiefly an eastern European species with a limited range from eastern Germany in the west to the Urals in the east, and from southern Sweden in the north to the Black Sea in the south (5).

4

2

3

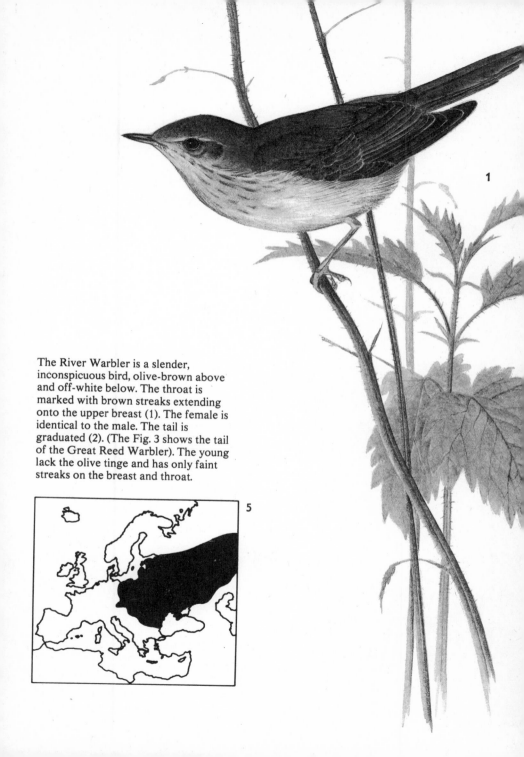

The River Warbler is a slender,
inconspicuous bird, olive-brown above
and off-white below. The throat is
marked with brown streaks extending
onto the upper breast (1). The female is
identical to the male. The tail is
graduated (2). (The Fig. 3 shows the tail
of the Great Reed Warbler). The young
lack the olive tinge and has only faint
streaks on the breast and throat.

1

5

Grasshopper Warbler
Locustella naevia

Sylviidae

The Grasshopper Warbler resembles the River Warbler in general habits: it is as secretive and mysterious in its behaviour, and is seen infrequently. Nevertheless, it is a denizen of a different environment than its relative; it lives in wet meadows with thick willow or alder thickets, at damp borders of ponds, in the alluvial regions of large rivers with small numbers of trees and bushes and less often in rape and clover fields. The voice of the male can be distinguished with practice from that of the River Warbler. It is a mechanical reeling on a single note, varying in pitch and delivered without noticeable interruption. The male Grasshopper Warbler sings remarkably intensely, especially at night. Grasshopper Warblers arrive at their nesting grounds in April—May. Pairs build a rather deep nest, mostly of leaves and stalks of grass, on the ground or nearby in a thick tangle of vegetation. Its walls are often intertwined with insect cocoons, and the nest is lined with dry grass and a small quantity of hairs. The eggs are similar to those of the River Warbler: there are five to six, and the incubation is shared by both parents for about 13 days. Both adults also rear the nestlings for 10 to 12 days. During August or September, Grasshopper Warblers leave for southern Europe, northern Africa and in some cases India.

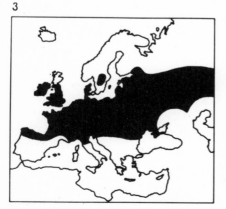

3

The Grasshopper Warbler is olive-brown above, with dark brownish streaks, and yellowish-white below, with light streaks, or merely with inconspicuous small marks on the breast (1). The sexes are identical. The young look like the adults but have more pronounced spots on the upper breast. The male sings from the top of a bush or a reed stalk, reeling away continuously for up to 2 or 3 minutes, all the while turning his head from side to side—which makes the sound louder or quieter, and gives the impression that the bird is moving from one spot to another (2). The Grasshopper Warbler is resident in a wide belt from northern Spain across Europe — excluding most of the Pyrenees, the Apennines and the Balkans — to south-western Siberia and Central Asia (3).

1

2

Great Reed Warbler
Acrocephalus arundinaceus

Sylviidae

The Great Reed Warbler is a bird with an extensive world distribution: it inhabits the whole of Europe (except Scandinavia and Great Britain), north Africa and Asia Minor. Other races live in the rest of Asia east to the Philippines and throughout Australia. Its favourite haunts are in thick growths of reeds and rushes. It is a typical migratory bird, returning in May. The nest is built by the female alone — who is a wonderful architect. Unlike the similar but distinctly smaller nest of the Reed Warbler *(Acrocephalus scirpaceus)*, it is situated above the water surface, most frequently 50 to 100 centimeters above it. It is made of strips of reed leaves and plant fibre, and lined with ears of reed stems. The female lays five to six greenish or bluish eggs with brownish or ash-grey spots. They are incubated by both parents for 13 to 15 days, and the hatched young are tended in the nest for a further 12 days. When they leave the nest, they are incapable of flying, but climb adroitly in the reed jungle, where they are fed by the adults for about 2 weeks. The nesting territory is small, 20 to 30 metres from the nest. Great Reed Warblers often rear young Cuckoos. The food consists of insects and their larvae, spiders and other invertebrates, picked up from marsh vegetation and the water surface. In September, they set off on their journey to equatorial and south Africa; Asiatic populations winter in south-eastern Asia. The Great Reed Warbler is a secretive bird, but immediately attracts attention by its loud, harsh, croaking voice, constantly repeating the phrase 'karre-karre—kit—kit'. The song is so loud that it drowns the voices of all the other reedmarsh songbirds. The singing male often climbs up a reed stem and sings very energetically, sometimes even at night.

The Great Reed Warbler is the largest of the European 'reed warblers', roughly the size of a thrush or starling. The coloration, which is the same in both sexes, is very plain and drab: the body is uniformly brown above and pale whitish below, with an indistinct pale stripe above the eye (1). The nestlings have the insides of their gapes orange-yellow, with a bronze tinge and yellow edges, and the tongue is marked with two longitudinal black patches (2). The nest is basket-shaped and up to 20 centimetres deep and is artfully woven among several reed stems, sometimes among green, fresh stems, and sometimes among the dry, old ones; this gives the impression that the stems actually grow through the walls of the nest (3).

Sedge Warbler
Acrocephalus schoenobaenus

Sylviidae

The Sedge Warbler lives at the edges of ponds and rivers thick with reeds, sedges, tall grass and shrubs, and also along ditches and in wet meadows with scattered osiers, or even far from water in corn or rape fields. It is absent from the Iberian Peninsula, but otherwise it is found almost all over Europe and across Siberia, approximately to the Yenisei River. It is a migratory bird, leaving for tropical Africa in winter. The nest is not 'tied' to plant stems as in other 'reed warblers', but merely pushed among stems of last year's reeds. It is built by both sexes, although the female bears the brunt of the work. The outer layer is of dry leaves of grasses or rushes, and the material gets softer towards the interior, which includes parts of reed stems, plant wool and hairs. The four to six almost uniformly coloured grey-yellow eggs, patterned on the blunter end with hair-thin streaks, hatch after 12 to 13 days of incubation. Following 13 to 15 days of parental care, the young leave the nest and stay in the area, where the parents feed them for a further two weeks. As soon as the fledglings become independent, the parents start a second brood. The nesting season lasts from May to July.The nesting territory is small, 20 to 40 metres from the nest; the male sings in its vicinity with great persistence, sometimes even at night. His song gives the impression of being hurried. In September—October, Sedge Warblers leave for their winter quarters, returning again in April or May.

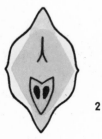

2

The upper parts of the Sedge Warbler are olive-brown, with dark streaks; the rump is russet-coloured and unmarked. The underparts are uniformly yellowish-white. The crown is streaked darker and there is a conspicuous creamy-white eyestripe — unlike the Aquatic Warbler *(Acrocephalus paludicola)* which has a conspicuous buffish streak through the dark crown (1). The sexes are identical. The nestlings can be identified easily from the bold markings inside the beaks, which are orange-yellow with paler edges, while the tongue shows two fairly long black patches (2). An excellent distinctive

3

characteristic of the Sedge Warbler is the male's song-flight, which frequently follows a burst of song and in which he soars up and descends obliquely with wide-open wings and widespread tail (3). No other 'reed warbler' does this.

1

Marsh Warbler

Acrocephalus palustris

Sylviidae

The Marsh Warbler can be distinguished from the other 'reed warblers' by several features: it is not so dependent on a damp environment as most of its relatives; it can be found not only in their typical habitats, but also in rape fields, corn and clover fields, in shrubbery belts, osier beds, in fields or in thick weed growths, often in nettles. Its song is less harsh and more musical and varied than in the other 'reed warblers'. Indeed, in some languages it is called the 'Dulcet Warbler', since its voice is rather sweet and melodious, reminding one of an Icterine Warbler. The Marsh Warbler is an excellent imitator of other birds: it can mimic Swallows, Partridges or other birds living in the neighbourhood. Marsh Warblers arrive at their nesting grounds from eastern Africa in May and soon after returning, they start building their nests in the typical 'reed warbler' manner, i.e. they 'tie' the nest to plant stems or shrub twigs, always above dry ground. They weave it together from dry leaves and grass stalks, plant fibres and gossamer. The eggs are bluish or greenish, lightly covered by large brown spots. The female lays four to five of them and both parents share the incubation for 12 to 13 days, and feed the nestlings for roughly the same time. Marsh Warblers are mainly insectivorous, but occasionally eat plant fruits. They are confined to Europe, ranging from Britain and France to the Urals. They are absent from the Iberian and Italian Peninsulas and almost everywhere in Scandinavia.

4

The Marsh Warbler lacks striking plumage features. Both sexes have the same coloration: they are dark olive-brown above, and paler creamy-white below. A faint light mark is discernible above the eye (1). They are very similar in appearance to the Reed Warbler *(Acrocephalus scirpaceus)*, from which they can best be distinguished by voice. In the hand, the Marsh Warbler

68

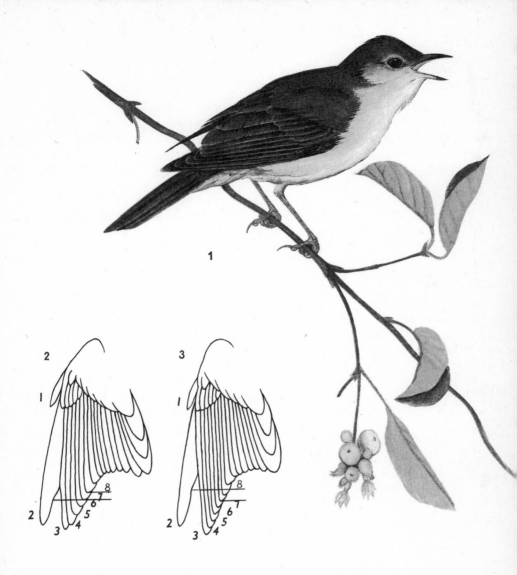

1

2   3

can normally be identified by the notch
on the inner web of the second primary,
which is situated above the tip of the
eighth primary (between the sixth and the
eighth primaries) (2). In the Reed Warbler,
the notch is lower than the tip of the
eighth primary (3). Even so, there is some
overlapping in these features, and others,
such as the comparative colour of the

interior of the gape, are not always
reliable. The young of the Marsh Warbler
have an orange-coloured interior of the
beak, and two longish black patches with
indistinct edges (4). The nesting territory
of the Marsh Warbler is small, with
a radius of 20 to 30 metres from the nest.
The male defends it energetically with
continuous singing, even at night.

Icterine Warbler

Hippolais icterina

The nest of the Icterine Warbler is one of the most attractive built by any bird. It is constructed exclusively in deciduous shrubs or trees and the twigs to which it is attached are solidly built into the walls of the nest. It is very clean and trim, and is made of dry grasses, pieces of moss, plant wool and insect cocoons, and decorated on top by white strips of birch bark. The beautiful pink eggs covered by scarce black dots lie in a soft lining of feathers and hairs. In late May or in June, the female lays three to five eggs and takes the greater share in incubation, relieved occasionally by the male. After 12 to 13 days, the young hatch and the parents feed them for another 12 to 13 days. Icterine Warblers rear only one brood because they leave at the end of August for their long journey to winter quarters in central and south Africa. They return in May to open deciduous woodland, gardens, parks and orchards. The Icterine Warbler feeds on insect and their larvae, but also eats various ripe plant fruits. Its voice is worth mentioning: the Icterine Warbler is a good imitator of other birds' voices, incorporating their calls into its own song. It usually repeats the main tune three times, and it can be easily recognized from its 'deh-deh-hoi, deh-deh-hoi' which is also repeated in the song. The Icterine Warbler lives mainly in the upper foliage of deciduous trees; the male sings very often, raising his crown feathers.

The Icterine Warbler is smaller than a sparrow, with brownish-green upper parts and sulphur-yellow underparts. It has a pale yellowish eye-stripe (1). Both sexes are identically coloured, and the young are similar, although the yellow is paler. The Icterine Warbler differs from the similar Melodious Warbler *(Hippolais polyglotta)* in its blue-grey legs. In the hand, the length of the wing (69 to 85 mm) and of the individual flight feathers are important features: the first primary is as long as, or a little longer than the coverts; the second primary is equal in length to the third and fifth primaries (2). The interior of the nestlings' bill is coloured similarly to that of the Sedge Warbler: it is orange-yellow with two black patches on the tongue (3).

3

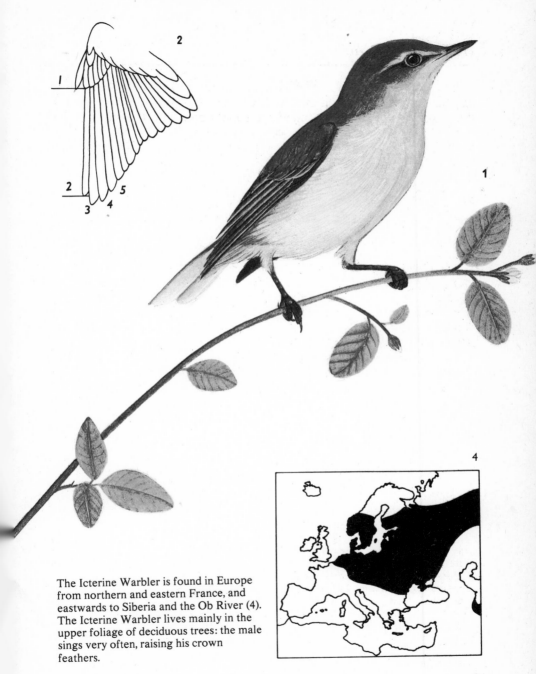

The Icterine Warbler is found in Europe from northern and eastern France, and eastwards to Siberia and the Ob River (4). The Icterine Warbler lives mainly in the upper foliage of deciduous trees: the male sings very often, raising his crown feathers.

Melodious Warbler
Hippolais polyglotta

Sylviidae

The Melodious Warbler is as good a singer as its relative the Icterine Warbler. Its song is slightly softer and this bird, too, often cleverly mimics songs of other birds. It sometimes sings in flight. It is a resident of south-western Europe, where it replaces the Icterine Warbler. In areas where both Icterine and Melodious Warblers occur, the males defend nesting territories against each other; apparently, such situations can also produce mixed pairs, but very rarely. The Melodious Warbler is found in similar habitats to the Icterine Warbler, i.e. deciduous woodland, areas covered by shrubs, orchards and gardens. It is a migratory bird, arriving in April-May, and nesting generally only once a year. The nest reminds one of that of the Icterine Warbler, but it is somewhat smaller and relatively bulkier. It is built by both birds, usually in shrubs. The clutch of four to five eggs is incubated by the female for 13 days; for a further 12 to 13 days, the young are fed on insects by both parents. From August to September, Melodious Warblers gradually disappear from the breeding grounds.

4

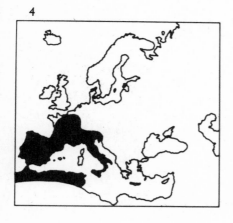

The Melodious Warbler is very like the Icterine Warbler but is distinguished from it by brownish feet; in the hand it has shorter wings (59 to 70 mm) (1). The wing formula is as follows: the first primary is more than 3 mm longer than wing coverts, while the second primary is between the sixth and the eighth primaries (2) in length. Both sexes are almost identically coloured, and the plumage of the young is very similar. The down is not developed in newly hatched chicks: as in other species of the genus *Hippolais* they are born naked. The eggs of the Melodious Warbler are pinkish, with small black spots (3). The eastern limits of its distribution are along a line continuing the eastern edge of the Italian Peninsula northwards to the Channel. The Melodious Warbler is also found in parts of northern Africa (4).

1

2

1

2

3

4 5 6 7 8

3

73

Garden Warbler
Sylvia borin

Sylviidae

The Garden Warbler is distributed throughout Europe, except the northernmost and southernmost parts. It is found eastwards as far as western Siberia. Throughout this extensive range, the Garden Warbler frequents deciduous and mixed forests with undergrowth, mainly forest margins and clearings, shrubs at river banks and around ponds, parks and belts of trees, both in lowlands and at higher altitudes. It returns from its winter quarters in tropical and south Africa in May. Soon after arrival, both partners start building a rather large but insubstantial nest in thick, low shrubs, often in blackberry or raspberry bushes. The outer layer is almost exclusively composed of dry, round grass stalks; the inner layer is made from softer dry grasses and sometimes hairs. The female produces four to five eggs, varying in colour from yellowish to greenish with grey or brown spots. Both parents incubate them for 12 to 14 days. At the age of 11 to 12 days, the young start leaving the nest, although they still cannot fly well. In the meantime, the male builds another nest, which is not actually used by the pair, as they rear only one brood a year. The Garden Warbler is mainly insectivorous, but in autumn, like other warblers, it also feeds on various berries or small fruits. At the end of August or in early September, the Garden Warbler migrates south to warmer regions.

The Garden Warbler is a very plain, drab-coloured bird, roughly of the size of a sparrow. It is simply grey-brown above and off-white below (1). The female and male are identical, but the juveniles have rather browner upperparts and the underparts more yellow-brown without the pale throat of the adults. The nestlings have a dirty red gape; its edges are yellow-white and the tongue has two longitudinal grey patches, very indistinct and sometimes entirely missing (2). The nesting territory is not too large, about 50 metres from the nest, in which the male sings very frequently from various places.

His pleasing song has rather long
phrases, and is presented in a rapid flow,
almost in the same key; it lacks the
outstanding flute-like tone of the
Blackcap. Pairs of Garden Warblers
often become foster parents to young
Cuckoos.

2

1

Blackcap
Sylvia atricapilla

Sylviidae

Of all the Sylviidae, the Blackcap is the most typical woodland bird. It is not confined to deciduous woods like the Garden Warbler, but is also found in coniferous, mainly spruce, forests in both lowlands and mountains; it is also found in field groves, overgrown gardens and parks. It builds an insubstantial nest, regularly situated in deep-shaded spots, chiefly low above the ground, made of tiny twigs, stalks and leaves of grass and lined with fine grasses, delicate rootlets and small quantities of hairs. Both parents share the incubation of the four to six uniformly brownish or thinly chocolate-speckled eggs for 13 to 14 days, and rear the nestlings for 11 to 13 days. Pairs with successful first broods nest for the second time in June or July. The male's song is loud and pleasantly musical: the Blackcap is one of the most acomplished songsters. The song is composed of a quiet warbling prelude, followed by a rich flute-like change of key. The song is somewhat slower than that of the Garden Warbler. The Blackcap is widespread in Europe and Asia, across to western Siberia, and in Asia Minor and on the north African coast. It returns to these regions in April, leaving in September and October when it sets out for the Mediterranean or to central Africa. Cases are known of Blackcaps wintering in the relatively cold climate of central Europe and small numbers winter regularly in Britain. This is possible because Blackcaps eat a higher percentage of vegetable food than other Sylviidae, e.g. berries of elder, rowan, viburnum or Virginia creeper.

2 ♀

The male has a grey-brown back and grey flanks with a well-defined black cap extending down to the eyes (1). Young males, usually until the autumn moulting, have a russet-coloured cap. The females are browner on the mantle and buff on flanks; the crown is also russet-tinted (2). The young resemble females. The nestlings have dirty red gapes with yellow-white edges and two longitudinal dark grey streaks with blurred borders on the tongue (3). Females lure predators away from the nest by pretending to be injured, as does the Barred Warbler and the Lesser Whitethroat.

Lesser Whitethroat
Sylvia curruca

Sylviidae

The Lesser Whitethroat frequents rather open country and avoids dense woodland. Its preferred nesting grounds include groups of bushes near a field path, or a smallish field grove; it can also be encountered at margins of woods and in gardens, orchards, cemeteries and parks; it is sometimes plentiful in parks of large cities. It arrives before all the other *Sylvia* species, usually in the second half of April. The males arrive a week earlier than the females and take up territories. Somewhere in a bush, usually at a height of about 1 metre, the pair builds their nest, distinctly smaller than nests of their relatives. The nest of dry stalks, stems and leaves of grass is very flimsy; its outer layers are often covered by spiders' webs. The four to six eggs are yellowish-white with rather large brown and grey spots, often forming a slight ring around the larger end. They are incubated by both parents until the chicks are hatched, which takes 11 to 13 days. The young are in the nest for about the same time. The parents feed them for some time around the nest, but before long are preparing to rear a second brood. The Lesser Whitethroat is less shy than its relatives, and responds rather indifferently to man approaching the nest. It often rears a young Cuckoo in its nest. During September and October, Lesser Whitethroats set out on the long southward journey to their winter quarters.

3

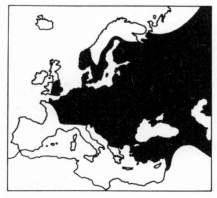

The Lesser Whitethroat is one of the smallest members of the genus *Sylvia*. It is dark grey above and dirty white below, with rich brown wings. The head is grey with dark cheeks, the throat is almost white. The legs are bluish or lead-grey (1). The nestlings can be recognized by the orange-coloured inside of the gape and two indistinct grey patches on the tongue (2). Its song is composed of two parts: a quiet, squeaking prelude, so soft that it can be heard only at close quarters, and the main song, consisting of a rattle on one note, sometimes bubbling, but in other males it is slurred. The Lesser

Whitethroat breeds almost all over Eurasia. In Europe it is absent from the western half of France, the Iberian Peninsula, a large part of the Apennines, the northern half of Scandinavia and northernmost Britain. In the east, its range reaches Mongolia (3).

1

2

Whitethroat
Sylvia communis

Sylviidae

The Whitethroat is found in similar locations to the Lesser White-throat, at the margins of woods and in clearings, hedgerows, orchards and parks, or in isolated groups of bushes in fields, and in grassy ditches or patches of nettles. It is readily distinguished from the Lesser Whitethroat by its song which has a series of short phrases and a rather louder final terminating rattle, ending on a rising note. The male sings from various vantage points, from time to time flying up while singing and descending back to the shrubbery. The nest is built by both birds close to the ground, mostly of dry grass stalks; it is often covered with cocoons or the webs of spiders. The clutch of four to six greenish, densely brown or grey-spotted eggs is incubated by both parents for 12 to 13 days. The hatched young are fed for 11 to 13 days in the nest. The adults rear two broods in a season, the first from May to June and the second from June to July. In September, White-throats set out for their winter quarters: European birds return to tropical Africa, while the Asiatic population migrates to India and Arabia. They breed in most of Europe, except the northernmost parts of Scandinavia, in a large part of Asia and on the northern coast of Africa, returning in April—May.

1 ♂

The Whitethroat is a rather plain-coloured bird: the male has an ash-grey head, a white throat, a grey-brown back and whitish underparts with a pinkish tinge. The wing coverts have striking rusty edges (1). The legs are yellowish to brown (2). The female differs from the male in being generally browner. The gapes of nestlings are dirty red with yellow edges, while the tongue bears two longitudinal dark grey patches with indistinct borders (3). Whitethroats often incubate a parasitic Cuckoo egg; the young Cuckoo is then reared instead of young Whitethroats. The female, like the female Garden Warbler, generally does not try to lure an enemy away from the nest by pretending to be wounded.

2 ♂

3

Barred Warbler
Sylvia nisoria

If we see a bunting-sized bird, in thorny bushes with its underparts barred rather like a hawk's, it can be only the Barred Warbler. Its bright yellow eyes, which give it an unusually fierce look, also suggest a bird of prey. And, true to its looks, it is extremely daring and aggressive at the time when it is rearing its young. It lives in open country with thick bushes, scrub or belts or shrubbery in fields, as well as thick grassy banks and forest margins. Unlike its relatives, e.g. Lesser Whitethroats, Whitethroats and sometimes even Blackcaps or Garden Warblers, it avoids the vicinity of human settlements. It is interesting that its nest can often be found where the Red-backed Shrike also occurs — a situation usually avoided by other songbirds. The nest is situated in sunny sites close to the ground; it is considerably larger than the nests of other warblers and is woven mainly of dry stalks and roots, and lined with hairs and plant wool. Both parents incubate the four to five grey-spotted, greenish or yellowish eggs for 14 to 15 days. They often sit on Cuckoo's eggs. At the beginning of the nesting period, the Barred Warbler is very timid, and often leaves the nest at the slightest disturbance. The nestlings are looked after for 14 to 16 days; later, the parents roam with them in the area. A second clutch is not laid, and during August the Barred Warbler leaves for east Africa, from whence it returns in early May.

2

The Barred Warbler is one of the largest warblers. The male superficially resembles a small Cuckoo or hawk: slate-grey on the back, with the flanks and underparts pale with grey transverse barring (1). The female differs in being much more brown on the back and less obviously barred below. The young resemble the female, but they have little barring on the underparts. Their eyes are dark. If the young are still in the nest they can be recognized by the orange, yellow-lined inside of the beak, with two dark grey elongated patches with blurred edges on the tongue (2). They have dark grey feet, while the young of the

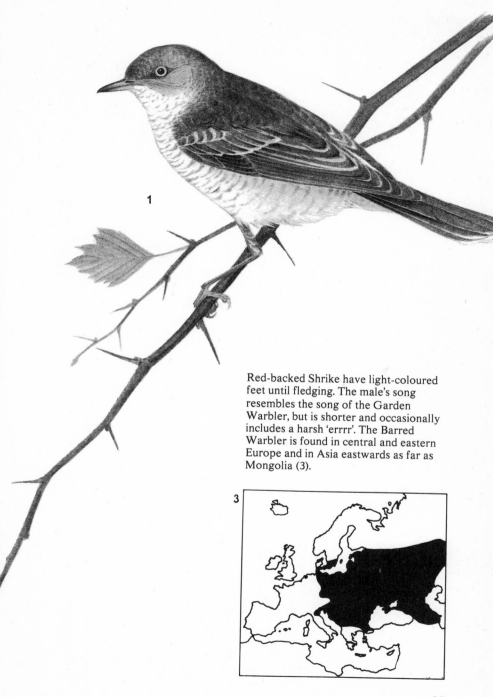

1

Red-backed Shrike have light-coloured
feet until fledging. The male's song
resembles the song of the Garden
Warbler, but is shorter and occasionally
includes a harsh 'errrr'. The Barred
Warbler is found in central and eastern
Europe and in Asia eastwards as far as
Mongolia (3).

3

Chiffchaff
Phylloscopus collybita

Sylviidae

Early in spring, generally in March, a simple, persistently repeated call can be heard from the treetops, sounding like 'chiff-chaff, chiff-chaff'. It is the song of the Chiffchaff, returning at that time from its winter quarters in southern Europe or north Africa, and settling in woods and groves with thick undergrowth and in larger parks or gardens. The female builds the nest and incubates the eggs alone; these are in a soft lining of tiny feathers and incubated for 12 to 14 days. The eggs are white, with minute russet spots, numbering 5 to 7. The female takes the greater share in rearing the young, for a period of 12 to 14 days; she feeds them almost exclusively on insects. When the first brood becomes independent a pair will usually start a second clutch. In September and October, Chiffchaffs leave for southern regions, but it is not uncommon for individuals to winter in various parts of Europe. The Chiffchaff is a European species with an extensive range into Asia, and it also occurs in parts of north-western Africa.

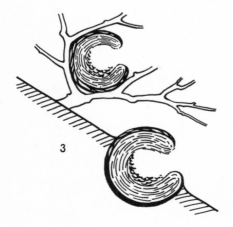

3

The Chiffchaff is a slender, inconspicuous bird, weighing 7 to 9 grams, grey-green above and dirty white below; the legs are dark, blackish-brown (1). The male, female and young are very similar in coloration. The arrangement of the primaries in Chiffchaffs is an important way of distinguishing them in the hand from the very similar Willow Warbler: the second primary is equal to or shorter than the 7th, while it is longer than the 7th in the Willow Warbler (2). The older chicks in the nest have dark or black feet and, unlike the Willow Warbler, are fed almost exclusively by the female, while the male regularly sings near the nest.

The nest looks like a domeshaped box: it is closed above, with a side entrance situated near the top. It is woven with dry grass, leaves and bark strips. The Chiffchaff constructs it either on the ground or close to it, e.g. in blueberry bushes, thick shrubs or low spruces (3).

Willow Warbler
Phylloscopus trochilus

The Willow Warbler is another common and typical European song-bird. Compared to the Chiffchaff, it has a somewhat more northerly distribution. In Asia, it reaches far into Siberia. It frequents sites similar to those selected by the Chiffchaff, but it prefers more open and sunny spots, including old gardens and city parks. The five to seven whitish eggs with tiny rust-reddish spots are incubated by the female for 13 to 15 days. Her mate helps her with the rearing of the nestlings, for 14 to 17 days in the nest and for some time outside it. His song is rarely heard during feeding. When the young become independent, the parents do not usually start a second clutch. Willow Warblers, like other *Phylloscopus* species, are mainly insectivorous, eating adult insects, larvae, pupae and tiny spiders. They pick them from leaves and the thin twigs of trees and bushes, or even from below the leaves — which they do by hovering under them — and also catch flying insects, spiders climbing down their webs, etc. In autumn, from September to October, Willow Warblers leave for central and south Africa; some winter in western Asia and Arabia. They return during April.

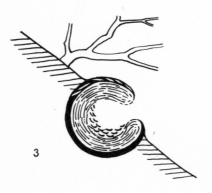

3

The Willow Warbler is difficult to distinguish from the Chiffchaff. It is similarly coloured, but it has a slightly more pronounced eye stripe and much paler legs (1). Nevertheless, the best identification feature of a *Phylloscopus* species is its song. That of the Willow Warbler is a slow, musical cadence with a curiously sad quality, gradually descending the scale. In the hand, the arrangement of the primaries is different from that in the Chiffchaff: the 2nd primary is longer than the 7th, while in the Chiffchaff it is shorter or of equal length (2). The domed nest is always

86

situated on the ground, usually on
a gentle slope, and it is carefully
concealed in clumps of grass. It is built by
the female from leaves, grass and moss
and lined with feathers, sometimes with
hairs in addition. The entrance is situated
at the side (3).

Wood Warbler
Phylloscopus sibilatrix

Sylviidae

Since all the *Phylloscopus* species have quite distinctive songs, the Wood Warbler can also be identified easily by voice. Its song is composed of a high, accelerating trill, resembling 'sip-sip-sip', and ends with a twittering 'sirrrr'. The male often sings during a gliding nuptial flight from tree to tree. The Wood Warbler is a forest-dweller, living in deciduous woods and rarely in conifers. It prefers oak and beech forests. The female builds a round covered nest with a side entrance, like that of the other *Phylloscopus* warblers. The nest is most often built in places where the vegetation is scanty, but even so it is extremely difficult to find: it is perfectly concealed under dry leaves or grass. The female alone incubates five to seven white eggs with relatively large, dark brown and grey spots. The chicks hatch after 13 days and are fed by both parents in the nest for 12 to 13 days, and for some time afterwards before they become independent. A pair rears only one brood a year, in May or June; in August—September, they migrate to the equatorial Africa. The Wood Warbler is a European species, inhabiting almost all of Europe except the Iberian Peninsula and the northern half of Scandinavia, and arrives on the breeding grounds in April or May.

3

The Wood Warbler is the largest of the *Phylloscopus* species. Unlike them, it has a sulphur-yellow throat and breast and a conspicuous, rather wide eye stripe. The abdomen is white, the upperparts are yellow-green and the feet are light-coloured (1). Both sexes are alike, but the young are rather duller in appearance. In addition, to the song, the arrangement of primaries is another distinctive attribute: the second primary is longer than the fifth and the first primary is discernibly shorter than wing coverts (2).

The nesting territory is usually
larger than in the other related
species, embracing a radius of 60 to 80
metres from the nest. The nest (3) is
unlike those of the Willow Warbler and
the Chiffchaff, never lined with feathers.

Goldcrest
Regulus regulus

Regulidae

The gentle 'sit-sit-sit' we often hear even in winter in coniferous forests is the call-note of the Goldcrest. Their song can be distinguished reasonably easily from that of the Firecrest: the individual notes are interchanged in differing keys, and the song resembles the sound 'tsi-tsi-dew-ee, tsi-tsi-dew-ee'. The Goldcrest is, together with its relative the Firecrest, the smallest of the passerine birds (the even smaller Hummingbirds are not passerines), weighing only 5 to 6 grams. It lives mainly in coniferous forests with spruces and pines, and usually builds its nest in these trees. It is often situated rather high, at 4 to 12 metres and is usually so cleverly concealed that it is invisible from the ground. The nest is chiefly built of moss, small twigs, plant fibres, animal hairs and feathers. During the first round of breeding in late April and May, the female lays eight to eleven yellowish eggs covered by indistinct beige spots; the second, June clutch is generally smaller. The female alone incubates them for 15 to 17 days, and both parents feed the nestlings for 16 to 18 days, bringing them small insects and their eggs and larvae, as well as aphids and spiders. They search for food like tits, carefully inspecting one twig after another. The Goldcrest occurs almost all over Europe and northern and central Asia. It is a partially migratory bird; northern birds set out southward in autumn and winter, starting roughly in October; they return to the nesting grounds in March or April.

2 ♀

The upperparts are olive-green, the underparts dull greenish-white. The wings are brownish-black with two small whitish wingbars. The male has an orange-coloured crown, bordered with black (1), while the female has a yellow crown (2), likewise edged with black. The young lack this head pattern; the head is olive-green like the back. The bill is fine and short and the nostrils are covered by a single feather. In relation to the miniature size of the bird, the nest is a massive construction hung below long side boughs of spruces or pines; the side walls of the nest are built into the vertical twigs and needle-leaves (3).

1 ♂

3

Firecrest
Regulus ignicapillus

The Firecrest is just as tiny and agile as the Goldcrest. It inhabits a similar environment, coniferous forests with spruces and pines. Its nest is also built beneath and onto branches of spruce or pine. It is made mostly of moss and the top is narrowed and with the rim overlapping the interior — an adaption to prevent the eggs or nestlings from falling out when the branches shake in the wind. The same arrangement is found in the Goldcrest's nest, which also has the shape of a sphere with a hole at the top. The female lays eight to ten eggs with a more pronounced reddish shade than those of the Goldcrest. The eggs of both species are in any case the smallest among European songbirds: they weigh approximately 0.72 grams and measure on the average 13.5 to 10.5 mm. The clutch of ten eggs then weighs 7.2 grams, which represents 144% of the female's weight. It is impossible to imagine where, during 10 or 11 days, she can obtain enough material to create more mass than she herself weighs — and twice in a summer too! The female alone incubates the eggs, but her partner helps to rear the young. Central European populations of Firecrests are migratory, leaving in October and returning in March and April. They winter in the Mediterranean area; Mediterranean populations are resident.

4 ♂

The Firecrest is very similar to the Goldcrest, but it is noticeably more colourful: it has a black stripe over the eye with a white stripe above it. The male's crown is fiery orange-red, bordered by black stripes which meet at the forehead. The shoulders are distinctly bronze-tinted (1). The female differs in having a yellow crown (2); the young lack this pattern, but the beginnings of a white stripe above the eye are already obvious. The song of the Firecrest is not so rich as that of the Goldcrest, and with practice he too can be told apart quite easily. It is a series of very delicate high notes, resembling 'si-si-si-see-see'. The distribution of the Firecrest is less extensive than that of the Goldcrest: it is found in most of Europe, except Scandinavia, in Asia Minor and in parts of north-western Africa (3).

In North America, another species is represented by *Regulus calendula*. The male has a striking red cap (4), while the female lacks it. These tiny birds have a white stripe around the eye so that they give the impression of having conspicuously big eyes.

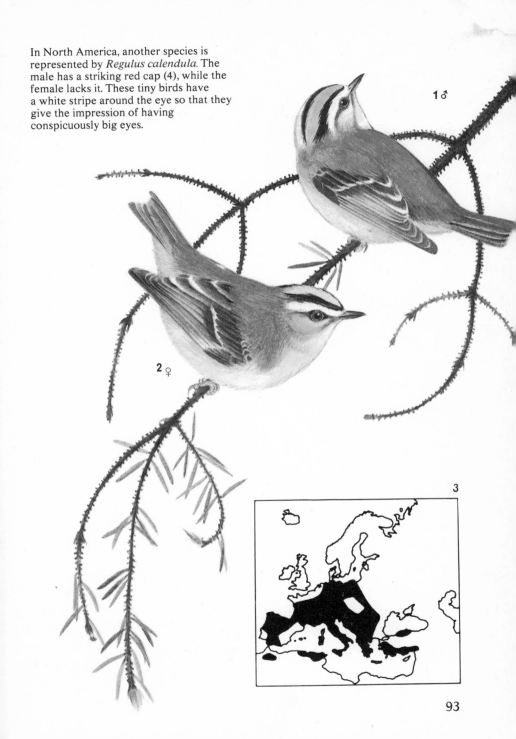

1 ♂

2 ♀

3

Spotted Flycatcher
Muscicapa striata

Muscicapidae

In parks, orchards, or lines of trees in forest margins or in the middle of villages and towns, we sometimes see a small grey-brown bird, typically sitting in a conspicuous upright position on dead branches, telegraph poles and wires or fence posts. Every now and then it flies up quickly to capture flying insects and immediately returns with the prey to the same or another perch. It is the Spotted Flycatcher, a bird found all over Europe, in north-western Africa and south-western Asia. Spotted Flycatchers return to their nesting grounds in late April and May. They build a nest in various hollows in trees, walls and rocky cavities, or just as readily on strong boughs or on rafters and beams in buildings. The nest is a solid construction of stems, roots, moss and various bits and pieces collected in backyards; it is lined with feathers or hairs. The four to six bluish or greenish eggs, covered by grey or reddish spots, are incubated mainly by the female, occasionally helped by her mate. The young are hatched after 12 to 14 days, and after a further 13 to 14 days leave the nest. Some pairs breed for the second time in June or in the first days of July, often using the same nest. In August and September, Spotted Flycatchers leave for their faraway winter quarters in Africa, from the north right down to the Cape of Good Hope.

2

The Spotted Flycatcher has greyish-brown upperparts and paler off-white underparts. The crown, neck and breast have darker streaks (1). Both sexes are identically coloured. Before their first moult the young are more strongly streaked on both the underparts and upperparts. The feet of the Spotted Flycatcher, as in all the Old World flycatchers, are weak and short, and are

1

used only for perching, not for running around. On the other hand, flycatchers are excellent fliers, capturing prey on the wing (2). They are aided in this by having bills which are wide at the base and enlarged by long bristles growing from the upper jaw. The song of the Spotted Flycatcher is very quiet and simple, easily escaping attention.

Pied Flycatcher
Ficedula hypoleuca

The Pied Flycatcher covers a vast range from the north African coast over the whole of Europe and western Asia to the Altai Mountains. It is absent only in some parts of western and southern Europe. On the continent its spring migration in April and May is particularly impressive: huge flocks of Pied Flycatchers appear in forests, parks and gardens for a few days. On the other hand, the autumn migration in August and September, when the birds leave for their winter quarters, is much less obvious. The Pied Flycatcher breeds once in a season, preferring old deciduous and mixed forests, but it also breeds in parks and orchards, and more rarely in coniferous forests. The nest is composed almost exclusively of dry grasses, soft roots and strips of bark; it is built in holes in trees and in man-made boxes. The male chooses the site, but the female undertakes the construction and incubation. She lays five to eight blue-green eggs in May and June; the young hatch after 13 to 15 days and are fed by both parents for 13 to 16 days in the nest, chiefly on flying insects and caterpillars. An interesting cross-breeding phenomenon may occur between the two black-and-white species of flycatchers in areas where both occur, either in larger colonies of Pied Flycatchers where a Collared Flycatcher appears, or vice versa. Cross-breeding between two species is a rare phenomenon in nature.

3 ♀

The breeding plumage of the male Pied Flycatcher is predominantly a pronounced combination of black-and-white (1). The word 'predominantly' is used deliberately: the coloration differs in central Europe (i.e. in the northern parts of GFR, GDR,

1 ♂

Czechoslovakia and Poland), where the males are grey-brown above (2), resembling females. In the field, it is often difficult to distinguish female or 'grey' male Pied Flycatchers (3) from female Collared Flycatchers. The alarm call helps: the Pied Flycatcher utters a brief 'bit-bit', the Collared Flycatcher an elongated 'seep-seep'. When determining the species in the hand, the most reliable features are the incipient white colour on the outer vanes of the flight feathers and the proportionate lengths of the second and fifth primaries — the fifth primary is longer than the second, (see pict. 3 of Collared Flycatcher).

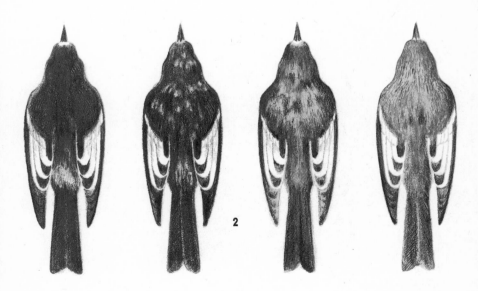

2

Collared Flycatcher
Ficedula albicollis

Muscicapidae

The Collared Flycatcher returns from its distant winter quarters in central and western Africa in late April or early May. Its habits resemble those of the Pied Flycatcher. It frequents open deciduous forests, and also parks, orchards and gardens. It nests in holes in trees, but equally often in man-made boxes, which can attract it, as with the Pied Flycatcher, into towns. It also nests in pure pine forests, if boxes are available. It needs a warmer climate than the Pied Flycatcher: it lives only in central and south-eastern Europe and in the westernmost parts of Asia. It does not occur at such high altitudes as the previous species. Soon after arrival, the male lures the female into the selected nesting hole not just by singing, but by various movements and visual signals: e. g. it repeatedly flies into the entrance of the nest and spreads its tail or wings, etc. The nesting territories are not too large, approximately only 50 metres from the nest. The breeding habits correspond almost exactly to those of the Pied Flycatcher. The nest holes are often surrounded by single, singing males. Together with males whose nests have been destroyed, they help to feed the young of other couples. The polygamy is a comparatively frequent phenomenon: one male often has several females. After fledging, parents and offspring stay for a short time near the nest, leaving for Africa at the end of August and in September.

5

The male Collared Flycatcher in breeding plumage looks like a groom in tails, complete with white collar (1). It is the collar that distinguishes this species from the Pied Flycatcher, as well as the white rump and the larger white wingpatches — the white starts on the third to fifth primaries. The second primary is usually longer than the fifth one (2), but these wing features do not apply as consistently as in the Pied Flycatcher (3). The non-breeding plumage of the male is

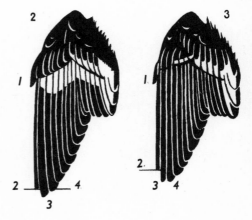

grey-brown, as is that of the female (4). Both black-and-white Flycatcher species are similar in their movements: the characteristic flicking of tail and wings (often of just one wing, which has a comical effect), and sitting on dead branches from which they take off to capture insects. The eggs of the Collared Flycatcher resemble those of the Pied Flycatcher; they are a blue-green colour (5).

Red-breasted Flycatcher
Ficedula parva

The Red-breasted Flycatcher is the rarest of the four flycatcher species living in Eurasia. Its typical habitat is hilly and mountainous beech forests, but it is also found in beech woods at lower altitudes, and less often in oak forests. The Red-breasted Flycatchers arrive at their nesting grounds in May, the males a few days before the females. The nesting territories are substantially larger than those of other related species — about 300 metres around the nest. Males are sometimes in the majority — the non-breeding ones sing very intensely until the end of June. The nest is built by the female of dry leaves, grass and fine roots, and sometimes of moss and hairs, most often in hollows, and less frequently in true holes, or simply between strong boughs of a tree. The female lays five to seven eggs; she incubates them for 13 to 14 days. The young, fed by both parents on small insects, stay in the nest for 14 days. The Red-breasted Flycatcher breeds once a year — in May or more often in June. After fledging, the birds remain in the nesting area for a short time only, and leave at the end of August and in September for their faraway south-Asiatic winter quarters in India.

3

The Red-breasted Flycatcher is at first sight not unlike a Robin. The male in breeding plumage has a similar brick-red patch (1) on the throat and breast; the female is olive-brown with lighter-coloured underparts (2). The males have this coloration even in non-breeding plumage, but young males sometimes lack the red patch until around the second year of age. The outer tail-feathers are pure white at the base, which is most noticeable in the

2 ♀

1 ♂

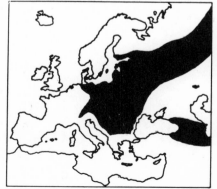

4

characteristic warning attitude, when the
birds spread their tails fan-wise and flick
them upwards, producing a loud
two-syllabled 'teedel-teedel'. The
Red-breasted Flycatcher ranges from
central Europe to the Urals and
eastwards to Kamchatka and Sakhalin.
The Caucasus and the Himalayas (4)
form isolated areas of distribution. The
eggs of the Red-breasted Flycatcher are
whitish, densely covered by tiny rusty
spots (3).

Stonechat
Saxicola torquata

Turdidae

The Stonechat favours sunny hillsides, stony slopes or dry meadows strewn with a few bushes, and, in Britain, heathland and coastal areas. The male sits in an upright position on an exposed perch — on the tops of bushes or tall plants, heaps of stones or telephone wires, and sings its grating song, which is slightly reminiscent of the song of a Black Redstart. Pairs rear two broods in a year: in April and then again in June—July. The nest is situated on the ground, always well-concealed under small bushes, clumps of grass or other vegetation. It is basically composed of dry grass, tiny roots and moss, and lined with soft grass and hairs, or sometimes with small feathers. The female produces five to six greenish eggs with small rusty spots, and incubates them alone for 13 to 15 days. The nestlings leave the nest after 12 to 14 days, although they cannot yet fly, and hide in the vicinity of the nest. Their rearing in and out of the nest is carried out by both parents, which bring them small insects and their larvae, spiders and worms. They search for food on the ground or catch it in the air. The Stonechat is a partially migratory bird: south European and African populations are resident, but others undertake spring migration in February—March and the autumn flight in October. The winter quarters are in equatorial and east Africa, or in Asia Minor or India, according to the breeding grounds of the birds concerned. The Stonechat is found in western, central and southern Europe, a large part of Asia and north-western and southern parts of Africa (1).

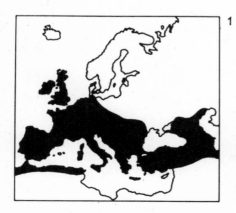

1

It is a colourful bird, a little smaller than a sparrow. The male has a black head contrasting with a large white patch on the neck and a bold russet breast. The upper mantle and wings are black-brown, while the wings have a small white patch (2). The female is basically similarly

3 ♀

2 ♂

coloured, but the black is replaced by
a brownish shade and the head and throat
are streaked darker (3). The tail-feathers
in both sexes are uniformly dark brown
to black. The juveniles are duller and
have dark bars on the back and breast.

Whinchat
Saxicola rubetra

The Whinchat is a typical migratory bird, arriving at the nesting ground in April—May in fields at road edges, in meadows with scattered shrubs and trees, and also in peat-bogs and mountainous plains. Adults observed in their nesting territories frequently fly from the top of one bush or tall plant to another. The nest is always built on the ground, usually in a shallow depression in the middle of thick vegetation, so that it is very difficult to find. It is built of dry stalks and leaves of grass, plant fibres and sometimes moss; the lining is usually only of the softest grass and, unlike the Stonechat's nest, lacks hairs. The female lays five to six eggs. She incubates them without her mate's assistance for 12 to 14 days. Only when the young are hatched does the male help to rear the family. The chicks leave the nest after 12 days, still unable to fly. Premature fledging is typical of both Stonechats and Whinchats, and of other thrushes which nest on or above the ground. Since the nests are easily accessible to many predators, scattering the young in the vicinity reduces the possibility of the whole family being lost. A single chick may fall prey, but not all of them, as could happen if they remained in the nest. It is therefore a protective measure. There is only one brood in a season. At the end of August and in September, Whinchats travel to their winter quarters in equatorial Africa.

3

The Whinchat is plainer-coloured than the Stonechat. It has a streaked back and crown, rusty-coloured underparts, a large white shoulder patch and white bases (1) to the outer tail feathers. The female is distinctly paler with the white shoulder-patch much less obvious (2). The young have streaked backs and breasts. The best distinguishing feature is a broad light stripe over the eye, characteristic of Whinchats of all ages. The eggs are a beautiful blue-green, sometimes delicately chestnut-spotted (3). The Whinchat is common in a large part of Europe — approximately from the Arctic Circle to northern areas of the Iberian, Italian and Balkan Peninsulas. It is also found over much of Asia (4).

2 ♀

1 ♂

4

105

European Redstart

Phoenicurus phoenicurus

Turdidae

If we hang nestboxes in an open deciduous or mixed forest, in a pine forest, or in a park or garden, they may well be inhabited by one of the most colourful songbirds, the European Redstart. It also nests in natural holes in trees and will readily use various cavities in buildings. From its winter quarters in equatorial Africa, the European Redstart returns in April and immediately becomes noticeable due to its lively temperament — energetic hopping and displaying of the rust-coloured tail — and the piping song delivered from elevated vantage points. After some time, it occupies a suitable cavity, which the female lines with tree leaves, grass stalks and leaves, roots, animal hairs and feathers. The European Redstart's nest is characterized by green moss woven into the upper rim. Shortly afterwards, five to seven eggs are laid in the nest and the female sits on them for 13 to 14 days. The chicks are fed by both adults for a further two weeks. Their diet consists mainly of insects, larvae and pupae. The breeding cycle is repeated once more during the summer. Redstarts often incubate a parasitic Cuckoo's egg. In September and October, they set out for their long trip south. The European Redstart is distributed throughout Europe and a vast part of Asia; it is also found in northern Africa.

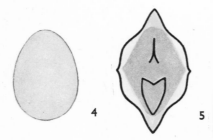

The male in breeding dress is really charming. He has a white forehead, black throat and cheeks, russet breast, rump and tail, white abdomen and grey-blue upperparts (1). The female is almost uniformly grey-brown, rusty-tinted below; the tail and rump are also russet-coloured (2). Juvenile birds are streaked on the back and breast, and can be mistaken for young Black Redstarts. Compared in the hand, the relative proportions of the primaries are important: in the European Redstart, the second primary is as long as or longer than the sixth; the third and fourth

2 ♀

1 ♂

3

1
2
3 4 5 6 7

primaries are the longest; the outer vane
is emarginated on the third to fifth
primaries (3). This applies to adults as
well as young birds. The alarm call of
European Redstarts is also distinctive:
a sharp 'few-id-tack-tack'. The eggs of the
European Redstart are bright blue-green
(4). The newly hatched young have dirty
ochre gapes with paler edges (5).

107

Black Redstart
Phoenicurus ochruros

Turdidae

The Black Redstart returns to its breeding grounds in March, and immediately becomes noticeable on account of its poor, rather unmusical song, delivered from roof tops or elsewhere on buildings. The majority of people know it as an inhabitant of towns and villages; few of them realize that the Black Redstart was indigenous to stony mountainous sites and moved to towns much later. It has taken readily to town life and in many areas is nowadays more numerous in such locations than in its original environment. Even birds resident in mountainous areas tend to settle near human habitations. The female builds the nest of dry grass, leaves and quantities of feathers and hairs under roofs of houses, barns and sheds, in wall cavities and in shallow hollows in trees. She gladly accepts an artificial, semi-open nestbox specially adapted for Redstarts. The five to six pure white eggs are incubated by the female for 13 to 14 days; the male helps only with the rearing of the brood. The young leave the nest before they are able to fly expertly, at the age of 12 to 16 days, but they stick to the area of the nest and the parents provide additional food for them. In a good summer, pairs rear two broods. Black Redstarts mostly feed on insects, spiders and centipedes, but in autumn they feed partially on fruits, e.g. elderberries, raspberries, etc. In October, they migrate to southern Europe, north-western Africa and Egypt; Asiatic populations winter in India and Arabia. The populations of southern and western Europe are resident.

4

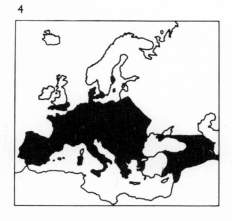

In its shape and movements, the Black Redstart closely resembles the European Redstart: it is as restless, constantly flicking its rusty tail. In other respects, it can be distinguished easily: it is almost completely grey and black except for the white areas on the wings. This is the male's coloration (1); the female is paler grey, without the white wing mark, but her tail is also rust-coloured (2). She is always darker than the female European Redstart. The young resemble the female, but they are darker, and slightly speckled on the upperparts. In the Black Redstart, the second primary is shorter than the

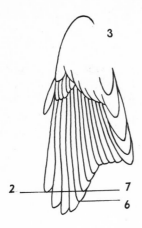

sixth; the third, fourth and fifth primaries are approximately of the same length. The outer vanes of primaries are emarginated on the third to sixth primaries (3). The Black Redstart is not as widely distributed as the European Redstart. It is found in western, central and southern Europe, in a belt from Asia Minor to China, and in a small part of north-eastern Africa (4).

1 ♂

2 ♀

Nightingale
Luscinia megarhynchos

Most people imagine the Nightingale to be the best songster among birds. Although the Nightingale sings during the daytime, it is by night that its concerts are most impressive. Every year many people undertake nocturnal trips into the countryside so as to enjoy this experience. The Nightingale is most often found in the margins of deciduous or mixed woodland, in overgrown parks and gardens or on banks of rivers or ponds, surrounded by a thick tangle of bushes. Nightingales return from their winter quarters in April or May. They arrive at night, the males first, which immediately start their song recitals; a few days later the females arrive, attracted by the night song of the males. In May or June, they build a concealed nest of dry leaves, grass, plant fibres and animal hairs, in a layer of dry leaves on the ground, usually in thick vegetation but sometimes in a fork of a branch or over a heap of dry branches. The clutch is complete when four to six olive-brown eggs are laid; the female sits on them for about 13 days. The young soon scatter, after some 11 days, and hide in the surrounding undergrowth. Until they learn to fly and hunt for food, they are tended by their parents. Unlike their arrival, their departure in August or September for tropical Africa is highly inconspicuous. The Nightingale feeds mainly on small invertebrates collected in rotting leaves; in late summer, it may take the fruits of some plants.

3

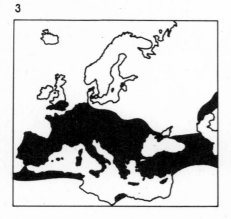

The Nightingale is known chiefly for its powers of song, not for its appearance. Many people would be surprised by its very plain plumage. The Nightingale is dull brown, darker above, paler below, with only the tail and rump russet-coloured (1). Juvenile birds are brown-streaked on the breast and back. If observed in the hand, the proportions of the primaries are relevant: the first primary is as long or longer than the wing coverts; the second primary is shorter than the fourth (2). Its song is worth a more detailed description: although the beautiful rich warbling of the Nightingale is taken for granted, it should be noted that not all the males sing alike. Some are genuine masters, others do not sing nearly so well. The capacity to sing is not inborn; the juvenile males have to learn by listening to the seniors, and the quality of their song reflects the proficiency of the older birds. The home of the Nightingale is in western, central and southern Europe, north-western Africa, western and central Asia (3).

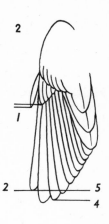

Thrush Nightingale
Luscinia luscinia

The Thrush Nightingale replaces the Nightingale in northern and eastern Europe. The boundaries of distribution of the two species overlap in central and southern Europe. The Thrush Nightingale occupies a large range in Asia, roughly to the Ob River (4). It is also a typical migratory bird, leaving its nesting grounds in autumn and moving to east Africa, and returning in April and May. It breeds in humid forests with lush undergrowth, or in river valleys or marshlands with thick shrub growth; it prefers wetter sites than the Nightingale. It constructs its nest in the shade of thick bushes, usually on the ground or close above it; the nest is so well concealed under surrounding foliage that it is almost invisible. The four to six brown eggs, incubated only by the female, take 13 to 14 days to hatch. The young stay in the nest for only 11 to 12 days, and while still unable to fly, scatter in the undergrowth. The male then helps his mate to rear them. The adults do not produce another clutch; the family stays together until the birds get ready for their long journey southwards. The Thrush Nightingale is as famous for its singing skills as its close relative the Nightingale. The difference in their songs can be detected only by an experienced ornithologist.

4

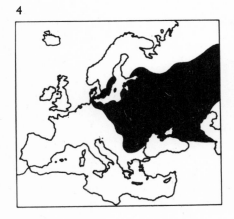

The Thrush Nightingale is very similar to the Nightingale: it has plain plumage, relieved only by the rusty colour of the tail; it is slightly darker above, with fine transverse bars on the throat and breast — this is its most significant distinguishing feature (1). Both sexes are alike. The proportions of the primaries are opposite to those of the Nightingale: the first primary is distinctly shorter than coverts and is also very narrow and pointed; the second primary is the same length as, or longer than, the fourth (2). The large brown eyes are another feature of Nightingales: their size indicates

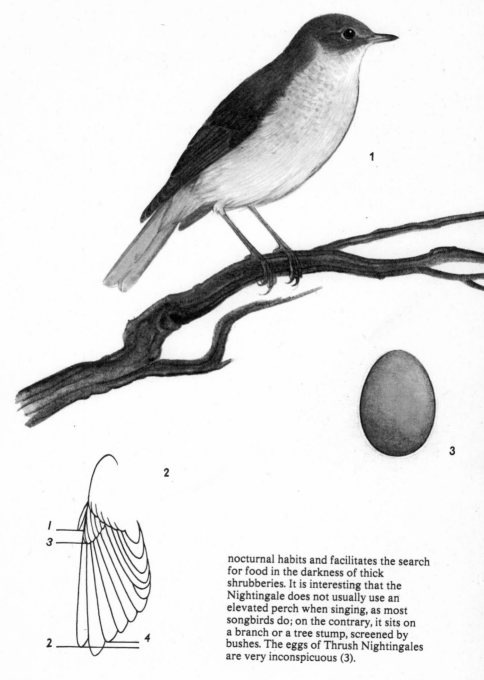

1

3

2

nocturnal habits and facilitates the search for food in the darkness of thick shrubberies. It is interesting that the Nightingale does not usually use an elevated perch when singing, as most songbirds do; on the contrary, it sits on a branch or a tree stump, screened by bushes. The eggs of Thrush Nightingales are very inconspicuous (3).

Bluethroat
Luscinia svecica

The Bluethroat is most widespread in the northern tundra, but also inhabits marshlands, banks of waters covered by reeds and bushes and river valleys liable to flooding. In central, western and southern Europe it is mainly encountered during spring and autumn migration, when the birds follow banks of rivers and ponds, or even tiny brooks and irrigation ridges. The autumn migration takes place in August — September and the spring flight in March or April, with such regularity that it can be estimated with an accuracy of 10 days. The well-hidden nest can be found as early as April, and from then on until July. It is usually situated in a scrape on the ground, protected by vegetation; it is woven of leaves of trees and grass, stalks, moss and roots. It contains five to six eggs, either brown or grey-green and brown-spotted. The young Bluethroats hatch after 12 to 14 days, and their rearing in the nest lasts as long. Both parents feed them on insects and larvae, worms, spiders and other invertebrates, which also constitute the mainstay of the adults diet. In autumn, when the Bluethroat travels to northern or north-eastern Africa, it occasionally eats the berries of certain trees and bushes.

1 ♂

In shape and behaviour, the Bluethroat reminds one of the more familiar Robin, but it is much more colourful. Two subspecies can be recognized by their coloration: *Luscinia svecica svecica* is the north European subspecies — the male in his nuptial dress has a blue gorget and a rusty spot in the centre (1); in the central European and south European subspecies, *Luscinia svecica cyanecula*, the male has a white spot in the blue patch (2). In both the blue gorget is separated from the whitish abdomen by a black and red stripe, and the rump and the tips of the tail-feathers are russet-coloured. In plain, non-breeding plumage, the bright colours of males

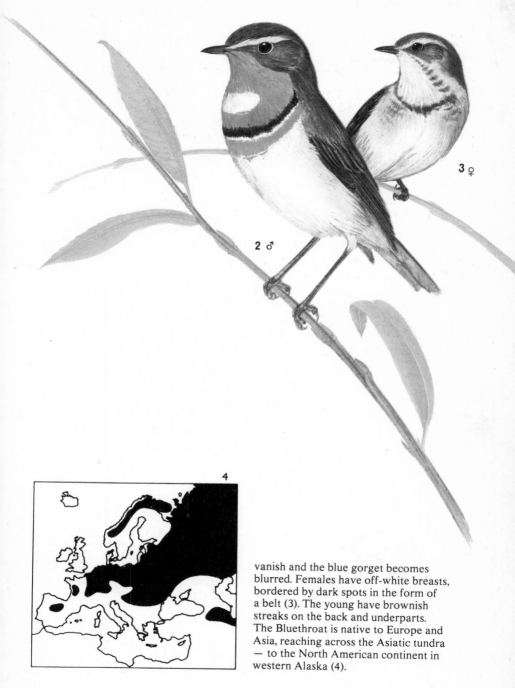

2 ♂

3 ♀

4

vanish and the blue gorget becomes
blurred. Females have off-white breasts,
bordered by dark spots in the form of
a belt (3). The young have brownish
streaks on the back and underparts.
The Bluethroat is native to Europe and
Asia, reaching across the Asiatic tundra
— to the North American continent in
western Alaska (4).

European Robin
Erithacus rubecula

The European Robin is a very agile, long-legged sprightly bird. When disturbed, it flicks its tail and bows conspicuously. Its favourite haunts are in the thick undergrowth of deciduous, mixed and coniferous woodland, although it is not shy of man's presence and may nest in overgrown gardens, parks or orchards. From March, the males occupy their nesting territories, staking them out by frequent singing. The construction of the nest is entirely carried out by the female, who is not too fussy in her choice of site. She builds it in a scrape on the ground, in a thick spruce, under roots, in a heap of dead branches, in a hole in the ground or a tree, or in a building or any kind of artificial structure. Dry leaves, plant fibres and green moss are the main materials; moss can also be seen in the outer layer. The lining is not too complicated, being composed of thin roots and hairs. The female lays four to six brown-spotted whitish eggs twice a year; the young hatch after 13 to 14 days. They leave the nest some 12 to 14 days later, unable to fly, and are looked after by the parents for some time. Both the young and the adults feed on insects of all ages as well as spiders, worms and tiny slugs; in late summer they eat various fruits. The European Robin is predominantly migratory, leaving for north Africa or southern Europe in September or October; most British Robins, however, are non-migratory. Individual Robins, mainly males, remain in central Europe over winter when they even produce quiet songs sometimes. British Robins sing regularly in winter.

Both sexes of the European Robin have olive-brown upperparts, with slightly darker wings and tail, and white underparts. The breast is a striking brick-red, this colour extending over the face to the eyes (1). The nestlings have green-yellow gapes with pale yellow edges (2); after fledging, they are brown-spotted above and below (3). The large, round eyes are very prominent: they help the bird to search for food in the darkness of thick bushes. The male's distinct song, quiet or loud and flute-like, is often heard until well after dark. The

3

1

2

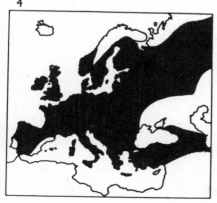

4

males are very hostile when defending
their territories, especially in spring, and
as soon as a rival takes interest in the
occupied territory, he is challenged and
driven off. It is interesting to note that the
male reacts chiefly to the red colour of
the breast of another bird; during the
spring he will attack even a dummy bird
if it has an artificial red patch painted on.
The European Robin is distributed
throughout Europe except nothernmost
Scandinavia: and in western Siberia, Asia
Minor and north-western Africa (4).

117

Wheatear
Oenanthe oenanthe

Although the Wheatear is a typical mountain bird, it is also found at lower altitudes — in sandy and stony fields, sunny fallow lands, sandpits and brick factories, railway or road embankments, and in locations overgrown with weeds. It has a world-wide distribution, inhabiting many parts of Europe, Asia, north Africa, North America and even Greenland. European Wheatears migrate in September and October to their winter quarters in equatorial Africa, returning in late March and April. They are fairly undemanding in their choice of a nesting site: nests can be found in heaps of stones, crevices in walls, holes in the ground or among the roots of bushes, and also in very unusual spots such as in rabbit burrows or under the sleepers of a working railway line. The nest is built by both adults and is made of dry grass, moss and roots. It is assembled rather loosely, but the inside is woven very carefully from a quantity of animal hairs and feathers, protecting the five to six uniformly green-blue eggs which the female incubates for about 14 days. The young Wheatears scatter from the nest after 12 to 15 days, but they are still unable to fly for several days more. Both adults bring them various insects, spiders, centipedes and small slugs. The food is usually caught on the ground, although insects can be captured in the air.

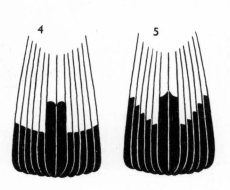

The male in his breeding plumage has a grey head and back, with black wings and tip of the tail, a bold black eye patch; the rump and most of the tail-feathers are white and the underparts buff (1). The female is similarly coloured, but is browner above and has the black replaced by brown or grey (2). The young differ from the female in having streaked upperparts and breasts. The nestlings have an interesting gape: it is yellow with a black stripe across the tongue (3).

The Black-eared Wheatear *(Oenanthe hispanica)*, a southern relative, is similarly coloured, but has much paler, more ochre upperparts; it occurs in two colour variants: black-throated and white-throated. Differences exist also in the coloration of the tail feathers and in the length of primaries: the Wheatear has black-tipped tail feathers, with the black on the middle pair extending further up the tail (4), and in the hand the second primary is seen to be longer than the fifth. In the Black- eared Wheatear, the black terminal band distinctly narrows from the outer feathers, although the middle pair are similar to those of the Wheatear (5); in the hand, the second primary is shorter than the fifth.

2 ♀

1 ♂

3

119

Rock Thrush
Monticola saxatilis

Turdidae

The Rock Thrush is an excellent songster: its song is composed of a mixture of flute-like notes, combined with melodies copied from the songs of other birds. The male often sings on rock walls, posturing with drooping, widespread wings. It is not restricted to mountainous areas; it is often just as much at home on dry rocky slopes, in quarries, or around castle ruins and city walls at lower altitudes. It is usually very shy and wary, living a highly secretive life and often escaping attention even when it nests in quarries where work is permanently in progress. The nest is built in rocky crevices, holes in walls, heaps of stones or in hollows under tree roots. It is a rather unsightly construction of plant stalks, roots, moss and grass, characterized by a lack of feathers or hairs. The female lays four to five light-coloured, green-blue eggs, and sits on them alone for 13 to 15 days. The young are nursed by both parents; they leave the nest prematurely at the age of 12 to 15 days, when they still cannot fly properly. Rock Thrushes return to their territories in April and begin to breed in May; the offspring leave the nest in June. They do not stay for long and during August and September leave for warmer regions in equatorial Africa and Arabia. The mainstay of the Rock Thrush's diet consists of insects, including their larvae and pupae, spiders and small slugs. Insects are picked up from the ground or caught in the air. The Rock Thrush also eats various fruits.

3

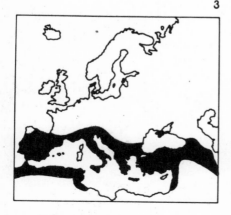

The male Rock Thrush is a beautifully coloured bird of the size of a Song Thrush. In breeding plumage, it has a slate-blue head, neck, breast and upperpart of the back, and is rust-red below. The wings are black and the tail rusty with brown central feathers (1). The conspicuous white rump is a distinctive feature in flight. The female (2) is mottled brown above, paler below; the young have a similar appearance. The male in non-breeding plumage loses his bright colours as the individual feathers become pale at the tips. The Rock Thrush is found mainly in central and southern Europe — the Giant Mountains (Krkonoše) in Czechoslovakia are at the northernmost limits of its distribution, north Africa and a wide belt across from Asia Minor east to Lake Baikal (3).

1 ♂

2 ♀

Mistle Thrush
Turdus viscivorus

The Mistle Trush is the largest Old World trush. It is found all over Europe (except northern Scandinavia), in western Asia, and in the Atlas area of Africa. It is chiefly a woodland bird and sometimes prefers coniferous trees, although it can be found in mixed woods or in old parks. The Mistle Thrush is not a purely migratory species: birds from the southerly populations are resident, while the northern ones move southwards in autumn. They return as early as February or March, and while the snow is still on the ground they start to sing from their favourite posts in the treetops. The Mistle Thrush is an accomplished songster; its song could be placed between the flute-like melody of the European Blackbird and the more staccato song of the Song Thrush. Owing to its occurrence in dark coniferous forests and to its pleasant slightly sad song, it is sometimes called 'Nightingale of the Black Forest' by local foresters. The nest is built by the female high in a tree, usually much higher than other related species. The male assists her and occasionally brings some building material. The full clutch comprises four to six greenish eggs with purple-grey and reddish spots, and it is incubated by the female only. After 13 to 14 days, the young hatch, and some 14 to 16 days later they leave the nest prematurely, as is typical of thrushes. Both adults feed them until they can fly well; they then start constructing another nest for their second brood. The Mistle Thrush feeds on insects, centipedes, etc; from late summer on into winter it eats various fruits and berries — blueberries, mistletoe, rowanberries, etc. Other thrushes have a similar diet.

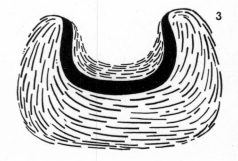

The Mistle Thrush is at first sight very similar to the Song Thrush. It is much larger and greyer above, with bigger and more pronounced spots below, reaching the abdomen (1). The wings are whitish below — an important identification mark in flight (2). Both sexes are identically coloured; juveniles are

2

1

yellow-and-black streaked above. The
nest consists of three layers: the outer
layer consists of dry grass, leaves and
twigs; the middle one of earth, which
soon becomes dried up and hardened
(characteristically, this layer can be seen
at the top of the nest), and the inner layer
is formed of fine grasses (3).

Blackbird
Turdus merula

Most people are familiar with the Blackbird. By its appearance and the tunefulness of its song, it enlivens even the largest metropolis, bringing into it a breath of the countryside. It was originally a woodland bird and many Blackbirds still remain in their native habitat. Some forest Blackbirds and those living in northern regions are migratory and move southwards and westwards. However, in autumn city Blackbirds and populations living in western and southern Europe are generally resident. Outside Europe, the European Blackbird inhabits north-western Africa and a belt from Asia Minor eastwards to China. Forest Blackbirds are extremely wary; although we may often hear them we hardly ever see them in the woods. They build their nests mainly in trees and bushes. City Blackbirds are not so selective, however, building everywhere — on eaves or house ledges, in large flower pots, on headstones in cemeteries or in piles of timber. The clutch numbers four to five eggs, and is incubated by the female for 13 to 14 days, and the young are fed by both parents for approximately the same time. The offspring then leave the nest and hide in the vicinity on the ground, where the parents continue to feed them. The female often builds another nest and rears a second brood. The so-called synantropization (urbanization) of Blackbirds has been taking place since the beginning of the century; it is explained by better living conditions that the birds find in cities, namely more easily available food and a milder climate. This has brought about the resident habits of city Blackbirds (they can easily survive the winter), that is, more frequent breeding and an increased number of pairs rearing three broods in a season.

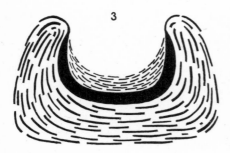

3

To describe a male Blackbird is very simple: he is entirely black with a yellow beak and a yellow eye-ring (1). The female is brown-black above and paler below, with a streaked throat (2). The European Blackbird is one of the first heralds of spring. While snow still covers the ground, Blackbirds start to sing their flute-like, slightly melancholy melodies from elevated perches. They are very busy songsters, starting before dawn and singing on into the evening, often until well after sunset. The nest is built by the female. The outer layer of grass stalks, leaves, moss and roots and the lining of fine grasses are connected by a layer of rotted plants mixed with soil, hardening more slowly than, say, the mud in a Song Thrush's nest (3). The eggs are bluish-green with regularly spaced, delicate rusty-coloured spots (4).

4

2 ♀

1 ♂

Fieldfare
Turdus pilaris

The Fieldfare differs from the other thrushes by often breeding in colonies: although some pairs nest alone, the majority gather in smaller or larger colonies, at times containing as many as thirty to forty pairs. The Fieldfare frequents hilly areas, older thickets along rivers or ponds, old parks and field groves, and forest margins, preferably near damp meadows. It is absent from dense forest. The Fieldfare is found mainly in northern and southern Europe and Asia. It is interesting to note that recently it has been shifting its range westwards and southwards. Fieldfares are partly resident, partly migratory. Northern birds and some of the central European ones migrate in autumn, mainly to western and southern regions. The nesting season lasts from April to July; in the more southerly areas, pairs rear two broods, but in the north there is only one each summer. The female sits on four to six eggs which are indistinguishable from Blackbirds' eggs, and 13 to 14 days later both parents start feeding the young. Rearing in the nest takes 13 to 15 days, and the young are fed for a further 2 weeks outside it. The diet consists of both animal and plant matter. In winter, flocks of Fieldfares feed chiefly on ripe rowanberries and other fruits. In the past, Fieldfares used to be hunted and their meat was regarded as a great delicacy. In some regions, they are prized even today as gamebirds.

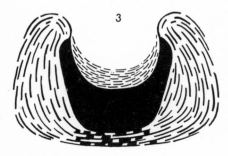

Unlike other thrushes, the Fieldfare is comparatively colourful (1, 2). Its most distinctive feature is the slate-grey head and rump, which contrasts with the brown back and black tail. The breast is russet-yellow and dark streaked; the spots and the yellow colour diminish towards the abdomen. The wings are white below. The female resembles the male, but the young are duller, the head and upperparts having a brownish colour.

The alarm call, sounding as
'tchak-tchak-tchak', is a very distinctive
feature. The male sometimes sings in
flight. The Fieldfare's nest resembles that
of the Blackbird. The outer layer is
formed by dry grass and leaves; the
middle one is made of mud, which soon
dries and hardens, the lining is of fine
grasses (3).

2

1

Song Thrush
Turdus philomelos

Turdidae

The Song Thrush is found over most of Europe and a large part of Asia. It frequents various types of woodlands, living more often on their margins than within them, and also parks, gardens and cemeteries. The nest is built in trees or bushes, but may also be found under roofs, in niches, in walls, and so on; it has recently become widespread in towns and cities. The majority of Song Thrushes on the continent are migratory: they leave in September and October for southern and western Europe or north Africa. They return in March and as they fly by night they may reappear unexpectedly on a chilly morning and surprise the local people with their loud and musical song. The males hold their concerts most intensely at dawn and sunset. The song can seem too sharp to some listeners: the Song Thrush loudly emphasises each individual phrase, which is usually repeated several times, and its song produces a staccato impression. The presence of the Song Thrush (and sometimes of the Blackbird) can be confirmed by its 'anvil' — a stone, stump or branches on which the bird breaks up the hard shells of snails, etc. Dozens of shells can be seen scattered round about. Song Thrushes begin to breed in April. The female incubates the eggs alone for 12 to 13 days. The rearing of the young in the nest is protracted to about 14 days, with the male helping. Food is collected on the ground; thrushes pick up everything they can as long as it is alive. When the first brood becomes independent, they start another one.

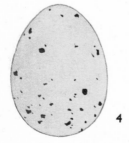

4

The Song Thrush is smaller than the Blackbird and is comparatively plain coloured: it is olive-brown above, including the wings and tail. The pale-yellowish throat and breast and the whitish abdomen are covered by dark brown spots (1). The female resembles the male, while the young have streaked backs. An important distinguishing feature in flight is the cinnamon-yellow

underwing (2). The nest of the Song
Thrush differs from that of other thrushes
in that it lacks a lining. It is made only of
two layers: the outer one of grass, leaves
and moss and the inner one of crushed
rotten wood cemented by saliva (3). The
four to six pale blue eggs with
widely-spaced black spots (4) are laid on
this bare surface.

129

Redwing
Turdus iliacus

The migration of northern Redwings can be detected even in large cities; if we go out at night and listen attentively, we soon hear the thin, far-carrying call 'see-ip' by which the migrating birds communicate. The real home of the Redwing is in northern regions; some pairs also nest in Britain and central Europe, and possibly, like Fieldfares, this species is spreading southwards. In the north, the Redwing is a typical taiga and tundra resident, in southern areas, it prefers thickets in damp locations or along rivers, and the margins of damp forests. In autumn, usually in October or November, large flocks of northern Redwings migrate to southern and western Europe or to north Africa. Many of them winter in central Europe, often together with Fieldfares. They return in March—April. Redwings build nests in trees or bushes; in the northern tundra they often construct them on the ground. The nest is built by both parents, and they share the duty of incubating the four to six eggs. After 14 days, the nestlings break the shell with the egg tooth, and in another two weeks leave the nest. The parents continue to look after them for some time.

5

The Redwing resembles the Song Thrush in size and coloration, but differs from it in the striking pale stripe above the eye and the chestnut flanks (1) and underwing, which is particularly noticeable in flight (2). The female looks like the male; the juveniles have spotted backs and lack the rich chestnut colour on the flanks. The nest is a substantial construction of grasses, leaves and roots, consolidateu by a layer of soil which reaches, as in the Fieldfare's nest, to the bottom of the nest, uniting it with the branches on which the nest is built (3). The eggs resemble those of the

Blackbird (4). Redwings are distributed in Scandinavia, Iceland, in the northern part of the U.S.S.R. and in Siberia (5).

131

Ring Ouzel
Turdus torquatus

The Ring Ouzel is not confined to mountainous areas; it often occurs in hilly places below 400 metres, and sometimes even lower (e.g. on coastal cliffs). It prefers coniferous mountainous forests, penetrating high into the dwarf-pine belt, but it also nests in beech woods of the bush type, and at the margins of forests of lower altitudes. It spends most of its time on the ground, searching for food and therefore seeks the vicinity of meadows, clearings and areas around uprooted trees. The Ring Ouzel is migratory, leaving for southern Europe, north Africa or Asia Minor in September—October. Individual cases of wintering in lower altitudes have been noted in central Europe. It returns in March—April. The nest is built by both birds; it is carefully screened in the thick branches of low spruces or dwarf-pine, but it can be often found even on top of a tall spruce. The nest is made of the same sort of material as that of other thrushes, but contains probably more thin twigs in the base. The full clutch numbers four to five eggs, resembling the Blackbird's, but the blue-green colour is more pronounced and the spots are brighter. Both partners share incubation, which takes about 2 weeks, and look after the young for another 2 weeks. Most pairs rear only one brood in a season; some pairs, chiefly in the southern regions, may rear a second brood. In its way of life, the Ring Ouzel resembles the Blackbird. It is fond of singing early in the morning and at sunset, often while on the ground. When it is searching for food among leaves, it turns and twirls the leaves with the same remarkable dexterity as the Blackbird.

3

The Ring Ouzel resembles the Blackbird, but the male can be distinguished easily by its white, crescent-shaped breast marking. It is not so black, but is rather brown-black, with the feathers, mostly below, tipped with greenish-white (1). The female is much browner with a paler, less conspicuous breast-mark. The young resemble those of the Blackbird, but have paler throats.

A darker race of the north European Ring Ouzel, *Turdus torquatus torquatus,* lives in the north; the white tips of the underside feathers are narrower and their middle lacks the white spots (2). In the central European Ring Ouzel, *Turdus torquatus alpestris,* the white tips on the underparts are broader, and many also have central white spots (3) in addition to the white tips. The Ring Ouzel occurs mainly in the mountains of central and southern Europe, but also nests in a large part of Scandinavia, Great Britain, Ireland and Asia Minor.

2

1 ♂

Bearded Tit
Panurus biarmicus

The Bearded Tit spends almost its entire life in extensive and thick reedbeds. It almost never leaves this environment, living a highly secretive and inconspicuous life. It is an agile bird, briskly climbing the reed stems, squeezing among them like a mouse, and matching any Reed Warbler in the dexterity of its movements through the reed jungle. In April, both partners build their nest in a thick tangle of broken rushes, or reeds, or in sedge tufts; it consists basically of leaves and inflorescences of reeds and aquatic plants, lined with feathers. The nest is usually situated close to the surface of the water. When the 5 to 7 white, delicately brown-speckled and streaked eggs are laid, both parents share the incubation which lasts 12 to 13 days. They attend to the young for a further 10 to 13 days in the nest and then for two weeks outside it. At the end of May or early in June they rear another brood. Bearded Tits generally gather into flocks for winter, feeding on seeds of aquatic and marsh plants, although the mainstay of their diet is insects and other small invertebrates captured in reedbeds.

2 ♀

The Bearded Tit is about the size of the Great Tit, with a long, graduated tail not unlike that of the Long-tailed Tit. The male is very handsomely coloured (1): he has a grey-blue head with long black 'whiskers', stretching from the beak to the throat. The whiskered effect is increased by the prominent feathers which form it. The upperparts are russet-tinged, the underparts slightly paler; the wings have two longitudinal white patches. The female lacks the grey-blue coloration on the head and the black moustaches (2); the young resemble the female, but they are black above and in the tail. The Bearded Tit's distribution in Europe and Asia is not continuous: it occurs in Britain and the Netherlands and from Spain across Eurasia to Japan (3). It is resident in southern regions, but northern birds undertake longer roaming trips in autumn. The Bearded Tit leaves its favourite reedbeds only during these winter eruptions.

3

1 ♂

135

Penduline Tit
Remiz pendulinus

Remizidae

The Penduline Tit is one of the most accomplished builders among all birds. Its nest is a small masterpiece and probably more famous than its builder. The nest has the shape of a mitten suspended on a thin vertical twig, with the entrance passage leading through the thumb. It most frequently hangs over water, and if it is situated on the bank, it is usually high. It takes about 14 days to construct the nest, which the male starts in April. Firstly, he makes the bag-like structure out of long plant fibres, and together with the female fills it with gossamer mixed with saliva. Before the nest is finished, the female lays five to eight pure white, elongated eggs, and together with the male builds a tunnel-shaped entrance, which constitutes the main feature of the finished nest. The male then leaves his mate and starts another nest, trying to attract another female. In one season he can succeed in breeding up to three times. The male and the female live as a pair only during the construction of the nest; the incubation lasts for 12 to 15 days and this, as well as the rearing of the young in their swaying cradle for 15 to 20 days, is all undertaken by the female. Some females probably breed twice a year. It is not easy to see the Penduline Tit. It usually moves in thick scrub or in the treetops, attracting attention by its high and protracted 'tseee-tseee' calls. The Penduline Tit is largely dependent on water: it is found mainly in pond areas or along rivers surrounded by thick vegetation, trees, and bushes. In southern regions the Penduline Tit is resident; birds from more northerly sites move south in the autumn. The diet consists chiefly of insects, but in autumn and winter it also includes seeds.

2

Both sexes are identically coloured: the head is grey-white, the back russet and the underparts yellow-white. A broad black mask extending from the beak to behind the eyes (1) is the most distinctive feature. This mask is absent in the young (2). The building instinct of the male is so strong that he builds not only nests in which females rear the offspring (12 to 18 cm high, 8 to 11 cm wide, with walls up to 2.5 cm thick [3]), but also 'cock's nests', which are never finished. This passionate builder can be lured by pieces of cotton wool hung on twigs. In

nests built early in spring the fabric is
mostly of fibres, and nests are
brown-grey; while nests built in May and
June are made almost exclusively of the
fluffy seeds of willows and poplars and
are almost white. The Penduline Tit is
predominantly an eastern and southern
European species, but also occurs in
a wide belt from Asia Minor east to
Japan (4).

4

3

1

Long-tailed Tit
Aegithalos caudatus

The Long-tailed Tit differs from other tits in its method of nesting: it does not nest in holes but builds its own nest in a tree or bush. The Long-tailed Tit is one of the best builders in the bird realm, and although it is one of the smallest birds (weighing 8 to 9 grams) its nest measures approximately 12 to 20 cm. It has walls 1.5 to 2.5 cm thick, woven almost exclusively of moss, lichen and a small quantity of plant fibres. It is so perfectly masked by bits of bark, webs and insect cocoons that it is hardly visible against a mossy oak trunk or in the thick tangle of needles in young spruces. It is equally incredible that the birds use a huge quantity of feathers (up to 2,000) to line its interior. The usual six to twelve eggs are incubated for 12 to 13 days, by the female alone. The chicks stay in the nest for 15 to 18 days and then fly out. They stay with their parents and have even been observed to help them with the rearing the young of the second brood. The same is done by pairs with no family of their own. The Long-tailed Tit is found all over Europe except the northernmost parts, extending its range eastwards to Japan and Kamchatka. It prefers deciduous and mixed woods, or young deciduous and coniferous forests, but it is also found in parks and gardens. It is almost exclusively insectivorous, and helps man by destroying dangerous pests, even in winter, when Long-tailed Tits gather in flocks. It ranks among the most useful birds, from man's point of view.

5

The best way to describe the Long-tailed Tit is probably to say that it is a 'white, long-tailed ball of cotton wool'. Owing to its long, graduating tail and the white, black and brownish-pink coloration, it can hardly be mistaken for any other bird.
Two subspecies are distinguished, according to head coloration, with a pure white head (1), and the central European *Aegithalos caudatus europaeus*, with a black stripe above the eye joining the

black colour of the back (2). Hybrids of
the two subspecies can be distinguished
by the incomplete or only lightly outlined
stripes. The young have black-brown
cheeks, neck and back, and lack the
pinkish hue of the adults (3). The nest is
a solid, oval, completely closed
construction with a small side entrance
near the top; both partners carry out the
building in about 15 to 20 days (4). The
eggs are white with fine red spots (5).

Crested Tit
Parus cristatus

As its name suggests, the Crested Tit can be recognized by its characteristic and conspicuous crest. It appears to be more cautious than other tits; the male sings relatively rarely, but when he does, he continuously frisks about, spreading and closing his crest. One call, sounding like 'si-si-choo-rrrr' is very conspicuous. The Crested Tit is resident in various types of coniferous forests; in southern and western Europe it also occurs in deciduous woods. The female starts the nest in a hole in a tree or a crevice in the bark, and sometimes even excavates a cavity in soft, rotten trunks. The Crested Tit rarely nests in man-made nestboxes. The cavity is lined with moss, dry grass and animal hairs, in which six to ten eggs are laid twice a year, firstly in April or May and then again in June. They are incubated by the female alone. The young hatch after 15 to 17 days and stay in the security of the nest for over 2 weeks. At that time, they are fed mainly on insects, plus their eggs, larvae and pupae, consuming quantities of bark beetles, weevils and other dangerous forest pests. The Crested Tit is a resident bird, roaming the countryside in autumn and winter and joining flocks of other tits. At that time, its diet is supplemented by the seeds of conifers, chiefly of spruce and fir.

2

The Crested Tit is not particularly colourful, but it is nevertheless an attractive little bird, thanks to its black-and-white crest which can be raised or lowered. The upperparts are grey-brown and the underparts dirty white, with a buff tinge on the flanks. The head is white with a black patch behind the eye, and a black chin (1). Both sexes are identically coloured. The young have short crests and the facial markings are more obscured. The eggs are white and red-spotted (2). The Crested Tit is resident almost everywhere in Europe except northern Scandinavia, the Iberian Peninsula and the Balkans (3). In Great Britain it is confined to a small part of the Scottish Highlands.

140

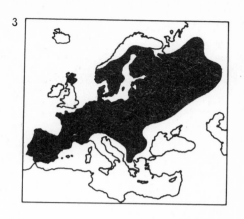

3

1

Marsh Tit
Parus palustris

Paridae

One peculiarity of the Marsh Tit is that pairs tend to remain together, even in autumn and winter and at any time when they gather with other Marsh Tits or join mixed flocks of tits. The Marsh Tit is a resident bird, not wandering far from its breeding area in winter. In spring, usually in April, pairs occupy their nesting territories where the females thoroughly inspect every likely hollow, although they are not too demanding: they will nest close to the ground or up to 10 metres above it. The female lays seven to ten eggs, which are white with a scattering of red spots, in a nest of moss, lichen, grass stalks and hairs. After some 14 days of incubation, undertaken by the female alone, the nestlings hatch; they leave the hole in 17 to 19 days, when they can fly. The male assists with the rearing and both parents continue feeding the young for some time. Unlike other tits, most pairs breed only once in a season. The diet consists of various insects and their eggs and larvae, mainly beetles with hard chitinous exoskeletons, aphids, spiders, flies, etc. In autumn and winter, the birds also eat seeds. The Marsh Tit's preferred habitat is deciduous and mixed forests, but it sometimes occurs in parks and gardens, though usually only around the edges of towns.

4

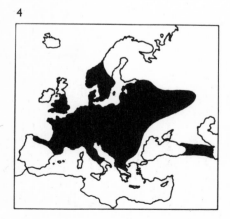

Both adults have the same, rather plain coloration: they are grey-brown above, dirty white below. Their most striking feature is the black, glossy cap, the small black bib under the chin, and whitish cheeks (1). In the hand, the Marsh Tit can be distinguished from the very similar Willow Tit by the characteristics of the underside of the tail: it is not so graduated in the Marsh Tit and the outer tail feathers are at the most 4 mm shorter than the longest ones (2); in the Willow Tit, the tail is strongly graduated and the outer tail feathers are more than 5 mm shorter than the central ones (3). The

young resemble the adults, but the top of the head is duller. Fairly distinct differences exist between the males' songs. The Marsh Tit's song is melodious and warbling; the Willow Tit's song is composed of five to six equally high, flute-like notes sounding like 'tsi-eh, tsi-eh, tsi-eh, tsi-eh, tsi-eh'. The Marsh Tit has an interesting distribution: it occurs in Europe and Asia Minor, and then thousands of kilometres away in the easternmost regions of Asia (4).

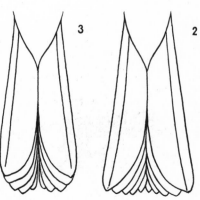

Willow Tit
Parus montanus

Paridae

The Willow Tit is probably the most widespread member of its family. Its geographical variation has not yet been fully explained: it forms several subspecies in Europe and Asia. North America is the home of a very similar species, the Black-capped Chickadee *(Parus atricapillus),* classified by some authors together with the Willow Tit. The Willow Tit frequents evergreen forests more often than the Marsh Tit; in the mountains, it may be found near the timberline and it also occurs in alder woods, and damp sites with bushes. The pair bond is not broken in autumn with this species either, and pairs stay together through the winter until spring, when the female starts excavating the future nest in a suitably soft, rotten trunk or stump. Since she is not as skilful a carpenter as the Green or Great Spotted Woodpeckers, and lacks a specially adapted bill, the work usually takes ten or more days. The spot can be easily recognized by the chips of wood dropped right under the entrance hole. The Willow Tit also makes its nest in old cavities. It is made of almost the same material as the Marsh Tit's nest, and its seven to nine eggs are also similar, as is the rest of the nesting programme. Pairs rear one to two broods in the period from April to June. It is found throughout Europe, except the southernmost and northernmost tips, and over much of Asia (1).

3

The Willow Tit closely resembles the Marsh Tit, but unlike that species it has a dull black cap, lacking the Marsh Tit's gloss. The black bib is fractionally larger. Each wing shows a distinct light line formed by the pale edges of the secondaries and the upper wing-coverts (2). Generally, though, these features are not always decisive: it is easier to identify the birds by their calls, a sharp and high 'pitch-u, tsi-eh' or 'pe-si-dadadada' in the Marsh Tit, and

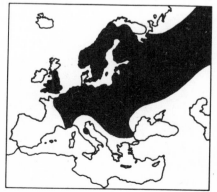

a low-pitched slurred 'dir-dir-dir' in the Willow Tit. The Willow Tit is a resident bird and only the northern birds travel south in hard weather. It differs from the central European subspecies by its greyer back and paler cheeks and underparts.

Northern Scandinavia is inhabited by a similar and larger species, the Siberian Tit, *Parus cinctus* which has a brown cap and a large black chin patch reaching to the dark coloration of the upperparts (3).

Blue Tit
Parus caeruleus

Paridae

The Blue Tit is a highly agile and active bird, as can be seen in the small winter flocks of this bird. They search every tiny crevice in the bark of trees, every thin twig, often rocking on them upside-down. In winter, their diet of insects is supplemented by berries and seeds. The Blue Tit is resident in deciduous and mixed woods, parks, gardens and orchards, in lines of trees along ponds and roads, or indeed anywhere where it can find trees suitable for nesting, i.e. sufficiently old, with holes. It readily accepts man-made nestboxes, and these are often erected by fruit farmers and foresters who know how many insect pests Blue Tits and other members of the tit family consume. The female brings a quantity of moss into the cavity and constructs a soft bed of hairs and tiny feathers for her clutch, which is usually ten to twelve eggs (sometimes, up to sixteen are laid). The little Blue Tits hatch after 12 to 14 days of incubation. The parents feed them assiduously, and the young leave the nest after 16 to 18 days. The adults feed them for another few days, and then begin to prepare the second clutch, which is usually smaller than the first. Blue Tits usually remain around one area and do not move far in winter. Like other tits, they are not equipped for migratory flights: they have short, round wings and are poor long-distance fliers. They seldom fly over bare, open country without sufficient cover. Only northern birds move south in winter so that Blue Tits could be called partially migratory.

3

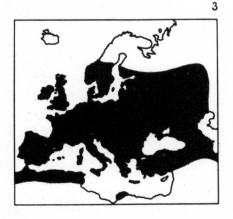

The Blue Tit attracts attention at once by its mainly blue coloration. The blue crown is conspicuous and the wings and tail are also blue. This colour contrasts with the yellow underparts, white cheeks and olive-green back (1). The female is identical to the male. In the young, the cap is more olive-green, the white areas of the head are yellowish and the

146

underparts are dirty yellow (2). In winter,
it is the most frequent visitor at
birdtables, together with the Great Tit.
The Blue Tit is distributed throughout
Europe, with the exception of northern
Scandinavia and the northernmost
regions of the U.S.S.R., and is also absent
from the Atlas region of north Africa (3).

Great Tit
Parus major

Paridae

The Great Tit is the best-known and probably the most popular tit. It lives in similar habitats to the Blue Tit; in parks and gardens in city centres it can be even commoner than the Blue Tit. In the mountains its distribution reaches the timberline. It does not move far in winter; only Great Tits from the north sometimes undertake movements which could be called migratory, e.g. birds from the Moscow area may appear in central Europe. The spring migration or wandering takes place in March—April and the autumn movements in October. Early in spring, the winter flocks begin to break up and Great Tits pair. Females build nests in cavities of all kinds: apart from holes in trees they nest in holes in walls, iron pipes, letter-boxes or discarded old cans or shoes. They like to occupy man-made nestboxes, lining with a thick layer of moss and preparing a deep hollow of hairs which is filled by white, red-spotted eggs laid at daily intervals. Whenever the female leaves the nest, she covers the eggs carefully and begins incubation after laying the eighth to tenth egg. She incubates without interruption for 13 to 14 days, and the male brings her food for the whole time. The young leave the cavity in 15 to 20 days when they can fly. The adults feed them for some time, then leave them and start another clutch, this time of only four to eight eggs.

4

At the first signs of spring, a bright sound 'tea-cher, tea-cher, tea-cher' resembling strokes on an anvil, is heard in forests and cities, repeated continuously. It is the song of the male Great Tit, drawing attention to himself as the courting period begins. He is a striking and colourful bird: the head, except for the large white cheek patches, is intensely black with a bluish gloss. The black colour runs as a broad line from the throat down the breast to the underside of the tail, dividing the lemon-yellow

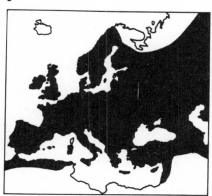

underparts. The mantle is olive-green, while the wings and tail are a bluish shade (1, 2). The female resembles the male, but has a narrower and shorter black line down her underparts (3). The young are duller in appearance and the black stripe is indistinct. The nestlings have ochre gapes (4). The Great Tit has a substantially wider distribution than the Blue Tit. In about thirty subspecies it occurs throughout all Europe, Asia and north Africa (5).

Coal Tit
Parus ater

The Coal Tit is a typical small bird of coniferous woodlands; if it occurs in mixed woods, it is almost always in sites where conifers prevail. In the northern regions the Coal Tit is migratory; northern Coal Tits tend to make long flights southwards in September and October, returning in March and April. Like the majority of other tits the Coal Tit nests in holes which are not so numerous in coniferous forests as in deciduous woods. People do not hang so many nestboxes in woods, but the Coal Tit, apart from natural tree cavities, makes do with rock crevices, holes under roots or abandoned mouse burrows; it nests in the walls or wooden structures of various forest buildings. Nests built on the ground are obviously often destroyed, either by various predators or by heavy rain. Pairs generally breed twice in a summer. The nest is solidly built of moss and animal hairs; all the work of building, and the incubation of the eight to ten eggs, is performed by the female. The eggs resemble the eggs of other tits and the young are hatched after 14 to 15 days; both parents bring them food after they leave the nest. The Coal Tit is also a most useful bird since it destroys so many insect pests. In winter, the mainstay of its diet is plant matter, mainly the seeds of conifers. In the tangled tree tops, the male makes himself conspicuous by his frequent, simple song, sounding like a repeated 'vidi-vidi-vidi'.

2

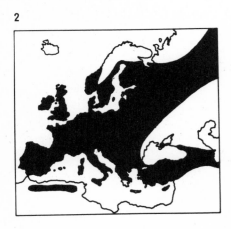

At first sight the Coal Tit looks not unlike
a small Great Tit, but a detailed
inspection reveals that it is really quite
different: both sexes have a black crown,
nape and bib, with white cheeks and
a white patch on the nape. The
underparts are dirty white, the upperparts
are grey-brown or greyish-blue (1).
Young Coal Tits resemble the adults, but
are duller with the black parts noticeably
browner. The Coal Tit occurs throughout
Europe, in a large part of Asia and in the
mountainous forests of the Atlas region
of north Africa (2).

1

Nuthatch
Sitta europaea

Sittidae

The Nuthatch is an interesting bird in many ways. Its favourite haunt is on tree-trunks and large branches, where it climbs about with the utmost dexterity, upwards or downwards (the latter movement cannot be performed by Woodpeckers or Treecreepers). Its amazing building instinct is another characteristic trait: the Nuthatch nests in tree cavities and adapts the entrance hole to its own size, narrowing it with mud mixed with saliva, so that only the builder can get inside (2). When it uses a nestbox, which it often does, the Nuthatch carefully stuffs the tiny gaps between the roof and the walls with mud. When the material dries the 'mortar' is covered with beak-marks. The female is the main builder and brings the nest material into the prepared cavity, assisted by the male. They almost exclusively use fine chips of pine bark (up to 2,500) or dry leaves in deciduous forests. If the Nuthatch manages to find even a single pine in the area it prefers its bark. A soft depression among the bark chips contains the clutch of six to eight eggs which are white with rusty-red spots. They are incubated by the female alone for 15 to 18 days; the male helps only with the feeding. The nestlings grow up very slowly, in comparison with other songbirds of the same size, not leaving the nest until they reach the age of 24 days. The adults take care of them after fledging and have no time to rear a second brood. The Nuthatch occurs over a large part of Europe (although not the northernmost parts of Scandinavia and the U.S.S.R.), as well as Asia, and occurs in the Atlas mountains in north-western Africa. It is fond of deciduous and mixed woods, parks, orchards and belts of old deciduous trees.

3

Both sexes have blue-grey upperparts, ochre underparts and a black eye stripe which is brownish in the young. The Nuthatch is a resident bird, scarcely ever moving far from its place of birth, even in winter. The birds roost in their holes in winter (2), but it is interesting to note that the male and female have separate sleeping quarters. Early in spring the male becomes conspicuous by his loud, almost human whistling as he stakes out the borders of his territory.

The North European Nuthatch, *Sitta europaea europaea*, differs slightly from

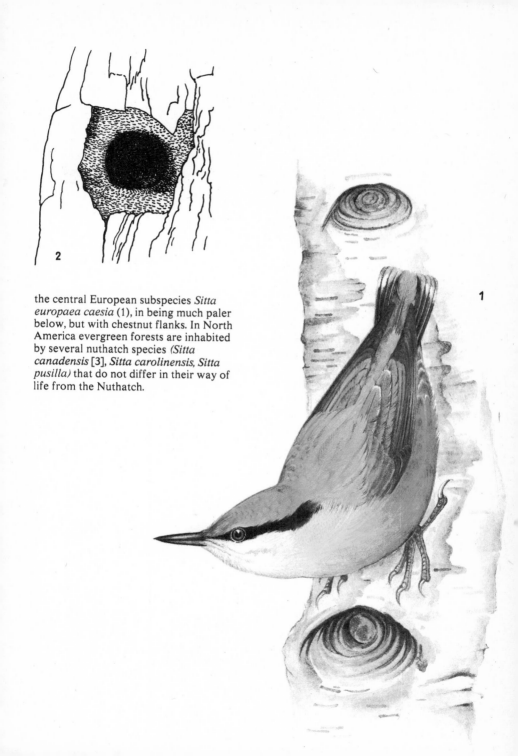

2

the central European subspecies *Sitta europaea caesia* (1), in being much paler below, but with chestnut flanks. In North America evergreen forests are inhabited by several nuthatch species *(Sitta canadensis* [3], *Sitta carolinensis, Sitta pusilla)* that do not differ in their way of life from the Nuthatch.

1

Treecreeper
Certhia familiaris

Certhiidae

The Treecreeper is also perfectly adapted for climbing on tree bark. It cannot climb head downwards like the Nuthatch, but it is equipped with long, sharp claws and with strong stiff tail feathers which serve as props, as in Woodpeckers. The Treecreeper has a world distribution: it is found not only in Europe and Asia, but also in North America from Canada to Mexico. It prefers coniferous and mixed woods, more rarely deciduous woods. It is found not only at their margins, but also deep inside them. The Treecreeper is not a typical hole-nester, but most frequently builds in tree crevices, behind cracked bark, or in wood stacks. The nest is a substantial construction for such a small bird: one notable characteristic of the nest is the quantity of tiny, dry often spruce twigs laid loosely in the selected cavity. The base is sometimes 40 cm high, topped by the actual nest of dry grass, strips of bark, feathers, hairs and spiders' webs. The female sits on five to seven eggs for 13 to 15 days; the nestlings are tended for 16 days. In June or July the female lays a second clutch, somewhat smaller. The Treecreeper, like the Short-toed Treecreeper, is a resident bird, joining winter flocks of tits and roaming the countryside.

2

The Treecreeper is a tiny, slender bird with a fine, down-curved bill. It has perfect protective coloration, so that the bird is invisible against the bark. The mantle has a tobacco-brown ground colour with light and dark streaks; the underparts are almost white, and there is a pale stripe above the eye (1). There are no differences in the coloration of the two sexes; the young have yellow-white underparts, and denser but less distinct markings on the back. The bill in the adults is slightly shorter than in the very similar Short-toed Treecreeper, but the

154

claw of the hind toe is usually
longer (8 to 10 mm) than the hind toe,
and less curved. The shiny, white eggs
have tiny red spots, mainly at the larger
end (2). When examining the bark, the
Treecreeper starts at the base of the tree,
climbing in a spiral to the top, and then
flutters down to another tree and
continues upwards with jerky
movements (3).

Short-toed Treecreeper
Certhia brachydactyla

In continental Europe, the Short-toed Treecreeper chooses a somewhat different habitat from that of the Treecreeper. It is also found in the margins of deciduous and mixed woods (it does not penetrate into forest complexes), but it prefers more open timber — field groves, parks, gardens or lines of old trees. Its habits and activities are almost identical to those of the Treecreeper: it climbs trees with the same adroitness, and concentrates on the same food. It is almost without exception an animal feeder. With its long thin bill it searches all the cracks and crannies in the bark, drawing out the hidden spiders and various insects, their eggs, larvae and pupae. During winter, when there is a shortage of this food, it also eats plant food, mainly small seeds. The nesting habits are similar and the nests are almost identical, very often in the same precarious locations, such as behind loose pieces of bark, so that it is risky to touch them. The eggs are somewhat different — red spotted on a white background, but the spots are larger and more numerous and the shell is mat. The female lays 5 to 7 eggs and incubates them alone. After 16 days of parental care the fledgelings leave the nest. Almost all pairs rear a second brood.

4

The Short-toed Treecreeper closely resembles its relative. It can be distinguished with difficulty by some not very obvious features. Its back is more grey-brown and the flanks have a brownish wash. The bill is slightly longer and the claw of the hind toe is shorter (6 to 7.5 mm) and more curved (1). Another important feature, visible only in the hand, is the characteristic dark patch inside the wing at the base of the first primary (2). (Pict. 3 — the wing of the Treecreeper). All these characteristics are usually insufficient for safe identification in the field. The most useful feature is the difference in song: in the Short-toed Treecreeper the phrases are shorter, sounding like 'ti-ti-titeroiti'; in the Treecreeper the song is longer, ending with a trill resembling that of the Blue Tit. Although the differences in songs are

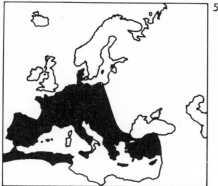

5

considerable it takes a lot of practice to
learn them thoroughly. A good field
ornithologist can advise and teach
beginners. The nestlings have a deep
orange gape with yellow corners (4). The
Short-toed Treecreeper has a markedly
smaller range than the Treecreeper and is
restricted to central, southern and
western Europe, north Africa and Asia
Minor (5).

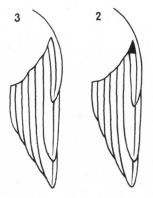

3   2

1

Corn Bunting
Emberiza calandra

Fringillidae

If we hear the jangling song of a Skylark-like bird a little larger than a Sparrow, delivered from isolated trees, telegraph wires or any other elevated perch in damp meadows or at field margins, it is the song of the Corn Bunting. This bird prefers lowlands and gentle hills, usually up to a height of 400 metres above sea level. The males start singing in March and April, in readiness for the females which reach the nesting grounds later. The female soon selects a shallow depression in the ground, on a meadow, in a clover field or on a slope, and builds a nest of grass stalks and leaves, rootlets and hairs. She lays four to five eggs and incubates them for 12 to 14 days. The hatched nestlings are nursed by the female only for the first 4 days, but then the male helps her. The young leave the nest at 9 to 12 days, before they can fly, and hide in the surrounding vegetation where the parents feed them. The Corn Bunting is sometimes polygamous. Some pairs rear a second brood; the breeding season lasts until June. Plant matter forms three quarters of the diet — mostly the seeds of various weeds, grasses and corn, but also including green parts of plants. The young are fed mainly on insects and other small invertebrates. The Corn Bunting is found in Europe from southern Scandinavia southwards, in north Africa, in Asia Minor and central Asia. It is predominantly sedentary; only birds from the northern regions gather in large flocks and travel to central and southern Europe. In winter it sometimes gathers in large flocks with Yellowhammers. If a mixed flock sits in a tree after being flushed, the Corn Buntings normally sit on top, while the Yellowhammers occupy lower positions.

The Corn Bunting is a visually unimpressive brown bird, darker above and paler below, with numerous longitudinal streaks (1) of a rich brown colour. The female is identically coloured, which is unusual in buntings. The bill has a characteristic shape, typical of all buntings: it is stout and conical, with the edges of the mandibles turned inwards and with a tooth in the upper mandible, which fits into a slot in the lower mandible. This enables the bird to hold and crush hard seeds (2). The eggs have

rather large dark spots on a reddish ground, and characteristic little veins, streaks or lines (3), as in all buntings. The Corn Bunting has a clumsy appearance as it moves on the ground, where it often flicks its tail. Before alighting it often hangs its feet (4) down in a conspicuous manner. Its song is a jangle of notes, sounding as 'tsik-tsik-tsik-shneerlrlrl'.

4

1

3

Yellowhammer
Emberiza citrinella

Fringillidae

The Yellowhammer is a common bird in meadows and fields with scattered bushes and trees, in field groves, in forest margins and clearings, in orchards and on the outskirts of villages and towns. From April to August it sings from vantage points in trees, bushes and telegraph wires, or on stones and lumps of soil. During this period it can be found all over Europe, except in the southernmost and northernmost regions, and in western Siberia; there is an isolated breeding ground in Caucasia. The males occupy nesting territories in April and defend them energetically. Few birds are as territorially aggressive as some of the Fringillidae. The females alone build the nest under overhanging clumps of grass, field boundaries or bushes. Some nests may, however, be situated high above the ground in bushes or even in trees. The clutch of four to five eggs, with the dirty white or reddish ground colour covered by black, brown or purple streaks and thin lines, is incubated by both partners for 12 to 14 days, and the young are fed for approximately the same time in the nest. After fledging, a second clutch is laid, and clutches of eggs found in July and August indicate that a third brood is sometimes reared. The diet is similar to that of the Corn Bunting. Yellowhammers from northern and north-eastern areas move to winter quarters in central and southern Europe; these migrations take place in March—April in spring, and in October—November in autumn. In winter Yellowhammers gather into flocks with other seed eaters — Greenfinches, Sparrows, Chaffinches, Bramblings, Linnets, Goldfinches and Corn Buntings. The winter flocks break up at the end of February. By this time the males can already be heard singing: their rattling song has one high note at the end — 'tsi-tsi-tsi-tsi-tsi-tsee'.

4

The Yellowhammer is not a shy bird; it often lets the observer approach to within a few metres. It hops on the ground, interposing its hops with walking, holding the body upright. It often flicks its tail and occasionally erects the feathers on its crown. The adult male has a beautiful yellow head with brown

2 ♀

1 ♂

3

markings, yellow underparts, rust brown on the rump and breast and dark brown wings, tail and back, the last covered by dark longitudinal streaks (1). The female is not so vividly coloured; is yellow-brown, and the breast and head are more streaked (2). The plumage of both males and females becomes somewhat paler in summer. The juveniles resemble the female, but are noticeably more streaked below. The nest is made of dry grass stalks, rootlets and thin twigs, and sometimes of leaves; the female carefully constructs a lining (3) of fine grasses and horsehair. The nestlings have dirty red gapes with yellowish corners (4).

Ortolan Bunting
Emberiza hortulana

Fringillidae

The Ortolan Bunting is a small, quiet bird. It does not defend its nesting territory as fiercely as the Yellowhammer; and several males may be found singing near each other. The song is reminiscent of that of the Yellowhammer, but the call is composed only of three to four notes, with the final one falling, so that the song has a melancholy effect: 'ti-ti-ti-ti-yer'. In many languages the bird has the name 'Garden Bunting', from the Latin *hortulana*. The name is not particularly appropriate since it does not nest in gardens; although in rare cases it may do so in orchards or vineyards. It shows a preference for gently rolling countryside with large fields and occasional trees and bushes, the margins of open woodlands bordering fields and dry, warm, stony slopes with scrub; it also frequents lines of trees along roads and paths. The nest is usually situated in a depression in the ground and is made of rootlets, bits of leaves, grass stalks and other plants, and is softly lined with fine plant material, horsehair and hairs. The four to five eggs are incubated by the female alone for 11 to 13 days. The eggs have a whitish or pinkish ground colour, covered by thinly spaced black-brown to red spots, dots and streaks. The young leave the nest after 11 to 13 days of parental care. Some pairs rear a second brood. The diet of the young and the adults resembles that of the Yellowhammer. After the breeding season, Ortolans gather in small flocks, travelling in August and September to their winter quarters in Africa or Arabia. They return at the end of April and in May. It is interesting to note that in many places in Europe, the Ortolans are declining in numbers. The widespread use of new techniques in agriculture, the elimination of scrub and other scattered greenery and the use of pesticides are partly to blame.

3

The Ortolan Bunting is slightly smaller than the Yellowhammer. The male has a greenish-grey head, neck and breast; the large yellow patch on the throat is divided by grey 'moustaches'. The underparts are cinnamon-brown and the wings, tail and back are brown with dark, longitudinal streaks. The bill is reddish, and there is a narrow yellow rim around the eye (1). The female has paler colours; her breast is streaked, but her throat is also yellowish, lined with dark spots, and

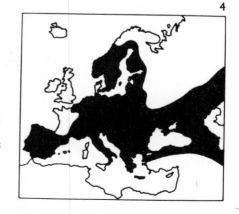

she has the grey moustachial stripe and pale eye rim (2). The young resemble the female. The nestlings have orange-red gapes with yellow edges (3). The Ortolan began to spread throughout Europe from the 17th century. Nowadays, it inhabits most of Europe except the northern parts of the U.S.S.R. and the British Isles, occurring in many isolated locations. It also occurs in central and western Asia (4).

Reed Bunting
Emberiza schoeniclus

Fringillidae

The Reed Bunting frequents an environment which is different from that of the other buntings. It prefers the damp banks of ponds or rivers, or areas covered by reeds, rushes, sedges and other marsh and aquatic plants, humid meadows with osiers, or peat-bogs. Here, the female looks for a suitable dry spot, to which she brings dry stalks and grass, bits of reed leaves and moss. She weaves the nest with these materials, lining it with grasses and animal hairs. The nest is usually situated on or close above the ground, always perfectly concealed under an overhanging tussock of grass, in a sedge clump, among broken reeds or in osiers. Nests may sometimes be found quite distant from water, in spots overgrown with nettles, lucerne, etc. The first clutch is in April and the second in June — July; both contain four to six eggs with the characteristic bunting pattern on a highly variable ground. The female mainly incubates alone for 12 to 14 days, but the male stays near the nest. The young are fed by both parents and stay in the nest for 11 to 13 days. When they leave it, they jump out into the grass or reeds and hide. The parents collect tiny molluscs, crustaceans and insects on plants, on the ground and even in water; later, they also collect plant seeds found near water.

The Reed Bunting is a restless bird, fond of sitting on reed stems, tall plants or the tops of bushes, flicking the tail, quickly spreading it and then folding it again. The song resembles the songs of other buntings, but it is very slow and broken: 'tsya-tit-tai-tsisiss'.

3

In spring the adult male has a black head separated by a white collar from the black chin and throat. The underparts are also white, with the flanks covered by fine streaks. Rich brown and black colours (1) predominate on the back, wings and tail. The female has a brownish head with dark spots, a buffish moustachial stripe, and dark brown streaks on the throat; the underparts are streaked (2). The young resemble the female. In autumn the male loses the black coloration of the head and throat,

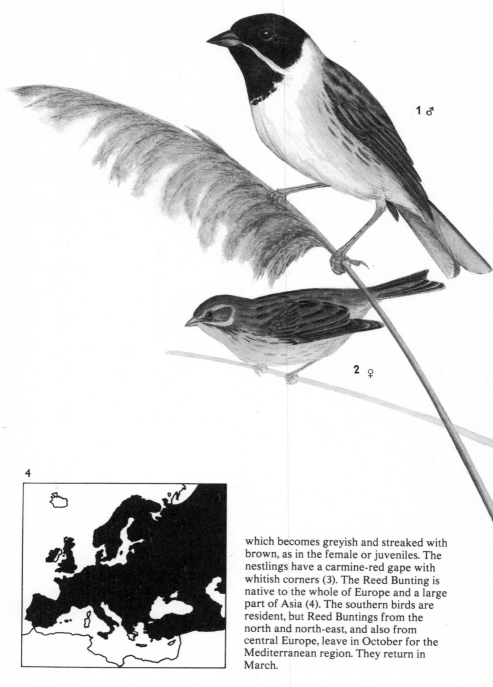

1 ♂

2 ♀

4

which becomes greyish and streaked with brown, as in the female or juveniles. The nestlings have a carmine-red gape with whitish corners (3). The Reed Bunting is native to the whole of Europe and a large part of Asia (4). The southern birds are resident, but Reed Buntings from the north and north-east, and also from central Europe, leave in October for the Mediterranean region. They return in March.

Chaffinch

Fringilla coelebs

Chaffinches are mostly migratory birds, although many of them stay in their nesting grounds over winter. It is chiefly the males that stay behind; this was noticed by C. Linné when he was giving the birds their scientific names — he gave the Chaffinch the name of 'bachelor' *(coelebs)*. Chaffinches have their winter quarters in southern and western Europe. In spring, they migrate in March and April; in autumn, in September—October. The flocks are generally divided according to sexes; the males arrive earlier. They immediately choose their nesting territories, vigorously staking them out by singing (resident males often start singing in February). After courtship, the female looks for a suitable nesting spot. The Chaffinch's nest is one of the neatest of all bird constructions: it is firmly woven of moss and delicate stalks, masked from the outside by lichens growing on the nesting tree, and by cocoons and webs, which make it almost invisible. It is lined by a soft layer of hairs, horsehair and down. The Chaffinch breeds twice a year, habitually building a new nest for the second clutch, although it sometimes rears both broods in one nest, especially if left undisturbed the first time. The eggs, averaging four to six, are of two colour types: reddish or bluish-green, covered by scattered, large russet spots, often with blurred edges, and various crooked lines. The incubation is carried out by the female alone. Chaffinches hatch in 12 to 13 days leaving the nest in another 2 weeks. The range of the Chaffinch extends from Europe to western Siberia, central Asia and north Africa. It frequents places where trees or bushes grow, parks, gardens, groves or forests, and does not avoid villages or towns. It is not too demanding in its choice of habitat.

2 ♂

The Chaffinch is one of the most trusting of birds, particularly in towns, where it is used to being fed by man. It moves with tiny steps on the ground, rarely by hopping, and flies swiftly with marked undulations. The male in breeding plumage has a blue-grey head and neck; the back is russet and the rump moss-green. The underparts are

4

1 ♂

3 ♀

brownish-pink. There are two white wing-bars, one wide and one narrow, and the outer tail-feathers are conspicuously white (1). In autumn, after the second moult the male's head is brown (2); by spring the brown edges of the feathers wear off and their grey centres become noticeable, producing the blue-grey colour of the head. The female is not so conspicuous; she is grey-brown (3) like the young. The gape in nestlings is carmine-red, richer in colour towards the centre, and the corners are whitish (4). Three-quarters of its diet consist of seeds; the rest of insects, mainly when the young are being reared.

167

Brambling
Fringilla montifringilla

Fringillidae

Annually, beginning in October, flocks of Bramblings undertake the long journey from their native lands to the south, wintering in central and southern Europe. Sometimes they arrive in small numbers, but in other winters their flocks number thousands. Together with other related birds, they gather in fields, meadows, fallows and near pheasants' feeding places, where they pick up grain and the seeds of weeds, birches and alders and certain berries. Beech woods are favourite haunts when beech mast is plentiful on the ground. In March and April they return to the north, where they nest either in pure birch or in coniferous forests mixed with deciduous trees. They usually build the nest in the fork of a branch, using moss and fine stalks with a lining of hairs and feathers. As with the Chaffinch, the nest is decorated externally by lichens from the tree on which it is situated. The female carries out all the work of construction and also the incubation of four to seven eggs. These resemble the eggs of Chaffinches. The young hatch after some 14 days and the male then begins to help with the feeding. They feed the young on a diet consisting mainly of insects, which they themselves eat at that time. In the short northern summers Bramblings manage to rear only one brood. Following the nesting period, families join together and begin to live in flocks again.

3

The adult male has a glossy black head and black upper back, while the breast and shoulders are yellow-brown to orange; the belly and rump are white (1). The wings are black-brown with two white bars and the tail shows white outer feathers. After the moulting of males into the non-breeding plumage, the uniform black colour of the head and mantle is broken by grey and brownish edges to

the individual feathers; the males at that time look more like females, which are more spotted and brown on the crown and nape, and have grey sides to the head and neck (2). Although Bramblings are different from Chaffinches, they resemble them in dietary habits, movement and behaviour. Flight is consequently similar, but Bramblings can be recognized quickly by the conspicuous white rump.

Serin
Serinus serinus

Fringillidae

The preferred habitat of the Serin is open country with scattered trees, open sites with groves, lines of trees, and overgrown water banks; it can be also found at woodland edges and often breeds in parks, cemeteries or gardens.

As soon as the male Serin appears in its nesting territory at the end of March or in April, it begins to sing energetically from an elevated perch, often on telegraph wires or treetops. The male is a very persistent songster; as he sings he sways to the right and left, which makes him look rather like a mechanical toy. He often delivers his creaky song during a ceremonial nuptial flight, swerving in arcs in a bat-like fluttering flight. After the courtship, the female finds a suitable spot in a tree or bush and builds a neat nest of fine rootlets, stalks, bark and lichens. She lines it with plant fibres, hairs and feathers so that the three to five tiny, bluish eggs with their few rusty-red spots are hardly visible. The hatched young are fed by both parents, which unlike other passerine birds do not swallow or take away the droppings but leave them on the edge of the nest; this is a significant recognition feature of Serins' nests. The chicks leave the nest after 11 to 14 days, and the pair start a second clutch. In September, Serins gather in flocks with other seedeaters and search for weed seeds, their favourite food. They also eat the seeds of birches and alders. Serins leave during October. Some individuals occasionally stay in central Europe until November, and in rare cases spend the winter there.

2

The Serin is a small-sized bird with a short, conical bill. The male has a bright yellow forehead, breast and rump. The top of the head, back and shoulders are yellow-green, with longitudinal dark brown streaks, and the wings and tail are black-brown (1). The female's yellow colour is not so bright, and the underparts are streaked from the throat downwards. The young are brownish and thickly streaked, lacking the yellow rump. If they open the bill it shines with a brilliant red colour; the edges are yellow-white (2). The Serin was originally indigenous to the Mediterranean region, i.e. north

1 ♂

Africa, southern Europe and Asia Minor.
In the early 19th century, it began to
spread in great numbers northwards
across the Alps. So far it has reached
southern Scandinavia and the Baltic
republics of the U.S.S.R. and has even
nested in England. Its distribution to the
east continued more slowly: it is rare in
Romania and barely reaches the borders
of the U.S.S.R. (3).

1968

1925

1875

1800

3

Greenfinch
Carduelis chloris

Fringillidae

In Europe, the Greenfinch is a resident, transient and migratory species. The birds from the north and north-east migrate in autumn to central and southern Europe; Greenfinches from southerly regions either stay on their breeding grounds or roam in their vicinity. Migratory populations return in March—April and immediately begin to nest. They prefer open country with abundant bushes or groups of trees, forest margins, parks, gardens or cemeteries. Like the other Fringillidae they require the proximity of open land where they can forage for food. The male is obvious with his distinctive song, often produced (as in the Serin) in a characteristic, bat-like ceremonial flight. Females are not too demanding in their choice of the nest site. In April, when deciduous trees and bushes are still bare, they like to build nests in conifers, but later also build in deciduous trees and bushes. The nest is fairly large and shallow, made of rootlets, tiny twigs and moss, and lined with soft rootlets, hairs, horsehair and feathers. The Greenfinch's nest often has wool woven inside and outside. The female sits on five to six eggs, russet or rusty-speckled and with a bluish ground for 12 to 14 days. The male feeds her during incubation. Both look after the hatched young, which leave the nest after some 14 days and sit on twigs near the nest. The young are fed mainly on plant food, partially digested in the parent's crop. The adults occasionally bring them caterpillars, spiders or insect larvae. Most pairs breed for a second time, and some even rear three broods.

3

The Greenfinch, with its plump body, large head and stout beak, and its clumsy hopping on the ground, gives the impression of a certain awkwardness. Of all the family of Fringillidae, it is one of the most trusting birds — this is readily seen in winter at any window-box feeding places. At that time, Greenfinches gather in flocks with other seedeaters and search for seeds in the fields. The male Greenfinch is bright olive-green; the

1 ♂
2 ♀

green colour is most striking on the rump.
It is slightly browner on the back and the
underparts are more yellowish. The wing
edges and the bases of the tail feathers
are bright yellow (1). The female is more
grey-green, and yellow areas are less
evident (2). The juveniles are streaked
above and below. Outside Europe the
Greenfinch is found in north-western
Africa, Asia Minor and central Asia (3).

Goldfinch
Carduelis carduelis

The Goldfinch is a highly mobile bird, never staying long in one spot, and is constantly sounding its call note (especially the 'steeglit' in the flight), immediately attracting attention. In autumn and winter, flocks of Goldfinches roam in fields, neglected meadows and fallows, eating thistle seeds or the seeds of burs and other weeds, or climb adroitly on the thinnest twigs of birches and alders and pick seeds out of their cones. Some Goldfinches wander around their breeding grounds, but others migrate to southern Europe in October and November. They return in March—April to nest in open country rich in trees, orchards, gardens or belts of trees and in thin deciduous and mixed woods. The nest of the Goldfinch can be found quite regularly in deciduous (often fruit) trees, usually at the end of a branch far from the trunk. The female uses fine rootlets, dry grass, moss and various plant fibres as building materials, intertwining the construction with insect webs and lichens from nearby trees, and thus making it inconspicuous. The nest is very thoroughly built with strong walls bent slightly inward at the top. In a cup lined with gossamer, hairs, down and horsehair, the female sits for 12 to 14 days on four to six eggs and is fed by the male who also frequently sings near the nest. Both parents bring the nestlings insects and later seeds softened in the crop. After 12 to 14 days, the fledglings leave the nest. The adults rear another brood and from later summer they gather with their families into flocks.

The Goldfinch is remarkably handsome with its red, black and yellow pattern, and can hardly be mistaken for any other bird. Both sexes are identical (1). The face is bright red and the crown and back of the neck are black. A creamy white band stretches between these two colours, forming a sort of a broad necklace. The breast bears a wide brownish band but otherwise the underparts and also the rump are white. The back is brown and the wings are black with a large golden-yellow wingbar; the tips of the flight-feathers and the tail-feathers are white. Juvenile Goldfinches lack the colourful plumage of the parents (2); the head is uniform brown and streaks cover

3

the back and underparts. Only the black wings with yellow bars show that after moulting the young will be as beautiful as their parents. The eggs of Goldfinches are whitish with fawn-coloured spots and russet dots (3). The Goldfinch is found throughout Europe (except the northernmost parts), across to western Siberia, and in Asia Minor, central Asia and north Africa (4).

Siskin
Carduelis spinus

Fringillidae

The Siskin shows a marked preference for coniferous forests, but it also nests in mixed woods and exceptionally in deciduous woodland. It is extremely difficult to find a Siskin's nest. During the breeding season Siskins are very quiet, and the female, choosing the site and building the nest, situates it very high and conceals it perfectly. The foundation is formed by thin twigs with a layer of rootlets, lichens and dry grass; all this is intertwined with the webs and cocoons of insects, and the inside is softly lined with plant wool, hairs and feathers. In April the female lays the first clutch and in June or July the second one. The eggs are bluish or greenish with russet dots or streaks, usually numbering four to six. The female incubates them alone for some 13 days, while the male feeds her. Both bring food for the nestlings for 13 to 15 days, at first consisting almost entirely of insects. The young soon begin to roam around; after the second brood is fledged both generations assemble in larger flocks and from August begin to wander in the countryside. Northern Siskins regularly travel southwards for winter, staying in central Europe or continuing to the Mediterranean. The mountain Siskins descend to the lowlands and appear in places rich in alders and birches, feeding on their seeds, which form the mainstay of their diet at that time. The return flights to the north take place in March. Courtship displays in flocks can be seen as early as February, when the male, singing, soars up in a fluttering flight and circles with an outspread tail. Siskins love bathing, even in winter, and sometimes they get so soaked that they cannot take off. Otherwise they fly very rapidly in an undulating manner, covering large areas at a considerable height; they can often be heard but not seen.

4

The male Siskin is completely green-yellow, with a darker back, streaked with blackish-brown, and the underparts rather yellower. The black-green wings have yellow bars and the rump and the base of the outer tail-feathers are yellow. The head is adorned by a black cap and a small black bib (1). The female lacks the black head

pattern and is more grey-green and distinctly streaked (2), like the young. The Siskin is an extremely agile and gregarious bird; the individual birds in the flock continuously call to each other so that the flock is constantly quietly chirping. The sharply pointed beak allows

them to penetrate the scales of alder cones; they grasp the ends of the thinnest twigs and pick out the seeds while hanging upside-down. The Siskin is found in central, eastern and northern Europe, Asia Minor and eastern Siberia (3).

A similar, more striped species *Carduelis pinus* (4) lives in mountainous coniferous forests from Canada to New Mexico.

Common Redpoll
Carduelis flammea

Fringillidae

The Common Redpoll has an interesting distribution: it inhabits predominantly northern tundras in Europe, Asia and North America, mostly in areas with birch and alder groves. A distinct subspecies lives in the British Isles, in the Swiss, Austrian and Italian Alps and in all the border-line mountains of Czechoslovakia, where it nests mainly in the dwarf-pine belt (4). Recently, the Redpoll has begun to spread to lower altitudes, nesting in the margins of mixed forests and those of spruce and pine, in birch, alder and willow stands in peatbogs and near water, and also in the parks and gardens of villages and towns. Redpolls are gregarious, forming small colonies. The nest is always situated low, and is made of thin twigs, dry grass and moss, lined with horsehair, hairs and feathers. The female usually lays four to six eggs, pale blue with a few brown spots and 'cloud patches'. She incubates them for 12 to 14 days, very closely, leaving only when man comes very close to the nest. She is fed by the male, who assists her industriously with the rearing of the nestlings; the care of the young takes 11 to 14 days. The food resembles that of the Siskin. In central Europe most pairs nest twice a year, which sometimes applies also to the northern Redpolls. Annually in autumn, approximately from October, Redpolls move southward, usually to central but sometimes also to southern Europe. In some winters they turn up in large numbers, generally stay until March and then return to the north.

3 ♂

The male is conspicuous with his red cap, carmine-coloured breast and tiny black bib. He is brown-grey above and off-white below, with the flanks and back longitudinally streaked; there are two pale wingbars (1). The female is more spotted and lacks the red colour on the breast (2); the young resemble the female, but without the red cap.
The subspecies *Carduelis flammea cabaret* living in Great Britain and central Europe is much darker and somewhat smaller than the north-European

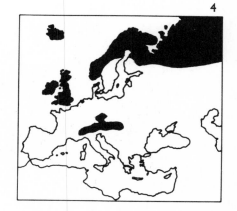

subspecies *C. f. flammea*. Redpolls are
very lively and gregarious birds; in flight,
we can hear the characteristic
'tche-tche-tche-tche' calls, which are also
heard in the twittering of males as they
sing on the wing.

The species *C. hornemanni*, the Arctic
Redpoll, is sometimes found among
Common Redpolls; it occurs in the
northernmost parts of the arctic tundra,
almost always nesting on the ground. It
differs in its whitish colour, especially the
rump (3), which is nearly white.

179

Linnet
Carduelis cannabina

Fringillidae

The pair bond in Linnets is much stronger than in other Fringillidae. One partner closely follows the other everywhere, not only in the breeding season but also afterwards; this admirable union seems to continue even in winter flocks. Linnets frequent hilly areas with field groves, bush-covered slopes and overgrown field boundaries, and open areas with low vegetation where the birds can forage for food. They also live at forest margins, in cemeteries, parks and gardens. The nest is generally low above the ground in a thick bush or in a tree. It is built by the female, but the male accompanies her faithfully. The nest is of stalks, stems, and rootlets intertwined with wool and fibres; the nest cup is lined with animal and plant wool. After 12 to 14 days of incubation, the young hatch from four to six eggs and leave the nest after a similar time. The eggs are incubated mainly by the female, although the male relieves her sometimes for a short interval; the young are reared by both. When the young become independent the parents start a second brood. In comparison with other related Fringillidae, Linnets concentrate more on seeds for their food. They eat few insects, bringing them to the young only in the first days of their lives. After fledging, Linnets gather in flocks with other seedeaters and stay in fallow lands covered by weeds. Some roam near the nesting grounds throughout winter, but others migrate to the south, mainly to the Mediterranean.

3

The male European Linnet is often considered to be the best songster of all the European finches. He usually sings from a bush or tree, but also sometimes in flight. He is handsomely coloured: in breeding plumage, the breast and forehead are carmine-red and the rest of the head and neck are grey; this colour gradually merges into a chestnut mantle and to the grey-white rump. The underparts are grey-brown and the wings brown-black with a white longitudinal patch; the tail is blackish-brown, with white edges (1). In autumn, the male has the red colour obscured by grey tips to

1 ♂

2 ♀

4

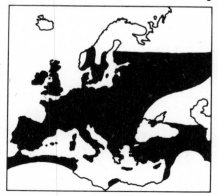

5

the feathers, but slow abrasion eventually causes the bright carmine colour to appear. The female lacks the red breast and crown and the chestnut mantle, and is quite unobtrusive-looking (2). The juveniles resemble the female. The nestlings have a dirty-red gape, whitish on the edges (3). The eggs of the European Linnet resemble the Redpoll's eggs and are very neatly spotted (4). The Linnet ranges throughout Europe from the south to central Scandinavia, and eastwards to western Siberia, and also occurs in north Africa, Asia Minor and central Asia (5).

Scarlet Grosbeak
Carpodacus erythrinus

Fringillidae

The Scarlet Grosbeak shows a preference for habitats near water, in lush overgrown valleys and the dells of rivers and brooks, bushes at pond banks, damp forests with thick undergrowth, and even neglected gardens and parks near human settlements. In mountainous areas it sometimes nests in the dwarf-pine belt. The male in the nesting territory is easily identified by his strong, whistling song, composed of several syllables, sounding as 'huit-huat-uat-yeh' from a distance reminding one of the Golden Oriole's song. He perches on treetops or bushes when singing. The Grosbeak is usually trusting towards man. The nest is started by the female in the second half of May, or later, generally low down and at the edges of larger groups of bushes. It is made of dry twigs, stalks and rootlets, lined with fine grasses and hairs. The incubation is performed by the female and the male feeds her on the nest. The young hatch in 12 to 14 days, leaving the nest in approximately the same time. They are fed by both parents, mainly on plant food but occasionally also on insects. Apart from seeds, the Grosbeak eats various fruits and pecks off tree buds. It is migratory, arriving at the nesting grounds in May, and leaving in late August or in September. Its winter quarters are from Asia Minor eastwards to India.

3

The Scarlet Grosbeak is Chaffinch-sized, but has a conical 'Grosbeak' bill. The adult male in spring has a rich crimson-red head, throat, breast and rump; the red colour is paler on the flanks and pinkish on the lower underparts. The wings and tail are black-brown and the back has a brownish tint (1). After the autumn moult, the male loses the red pigment and resembles the female, which is olive-brown above and whitish below, with darker longitudinal streaks on the breast and back (2). The young resemble the female, but have duller and darker colours. Until the second year of their life, males look like females, lacking the red plumage, although they are able to breed in this incomplete plumage. The clutch numbers four to six intensely blue-green eggs with scattered, near-black spots, concentrated at the larger end (3). The Scarlet

1 ♂

2 ♀

4

Grosbeak is found from eastern Europe
to western Siberia. The western boundary
passes through Denmark and Germany
(Mecklenburg), the southern one through
Czechoslovakia, and the northern one
through southern Finland. It also occurs
in the mountains of Asia Minor. Recently,
an expansion has been noted from the
north-east towards the south and
west (4).

183

Common Crossbill
Loxia curvirostra

Fringillidae

Crossbills are often referred to as the parrots of coniferous forests — this is because they are extremely agile in trees and hang upside-down on cones, sometimes snipping these off with their bills. They then carry them to another tree to hold them on a branch with their feet while they pick out the seeds. They throw away the cones without ever extracting all the seeds. Their flight is rapid and undulating, accompanied by loud 'kip-kip' calls. By contrast, they are quite clumsy on the ground, moving in awkward hops. Common Crossbills breed regularly even in winter. They can produce offspring in any month, but prefer January to April. It is quite clear that their breeding habits depend on the availability of their main food — ripe cones. The Crossbill's nest is a substantial construction with walls up to 3 cm thick, providing excellent insulation. It is always situated in coniferous trees, high up and close to the trunk, or in a tangle of peripheral branches. The nest is built solely by the female using coniferous twigs, stalks, moss, lichens and fine rootlets; the male accompanies his mate in the collecting and carrying of materials. The female lays three to four greenish eggs with sparse russet spots. She sits on them after laying the first egg, and hardly leaves the nest for 14 to 16 days. She continues to be fed by the male in the first days after hatching, but flies out to search for her own food as well. After some 14 days the young leave the nest, but stay with the parents for some time and later gather with other families. Pairs sometimes nest twice in the same season. The principal habitat of Crossbills is in spruce and fir forests up to the timberline in the mountains. Crossbills simply move to areas where cones are plentiful. They may swarm in a region one year, and then not be seen there at all the following season. If more cones ripen in lowland sites, Crossbills descend from the mountains. When the cone harvest in the continuous forests of the north and north-east is poor, huge flocks of Crossbills invade Europe and appear in every area where they can find food. These movements are called 'invasions'.

The adult male is almost completely brick-red; only the wings and tail are brown (1). Many yellow-green males also exist (they are not just young males as was once believed; it was discovered that the originally red male can moult to a yellow coloration). The coloration is influenced by the quantity of available food and by the bird's physical condition. The female is yellow-green, with dark longitudinal streaks and a yellowish rump (2). The young are olive-brown above

2 ♀

1 ♂

3

4

and grey-white below, and heavily streaked (3). The Common Crossbill inhabits the forests of Europe, Asia, North America and north-western Africa (4).

Two-barred Crossbill
Loxia leucoptera

Fringillidae

The Two-barred Crossbill frequents the coniferous forests of the north, showing a strong preference for larch woods, which provide its basic food — the seeds from larch cones. It extracts the seeds of these and other conifers, the seeds of other plants and partially feeds on insects. The nest is built in conifers by the female, in a manner similar to that of the Common Crossbill, although it is smaller. The whole course of nesting is also similar, but the breeding period is in spring and summer, from March to June. In the first days of life, both mandibles fit together as in other birds, but later they cross. The position of the upper mandible relative to the lower one (i.e. whether it is to the right or left) seems to be incidental; both forms of the beak occur equally often, even in chicks from the same nest. The same applies to the Common Crossbill. The crossing, taking place after the third week of life, is later perfected by the picking of seeds from cones: Crossbills push the crossed mandibles between the scales of cones, open them and pick out the seeds with the tongue. After the fledging of the young, families begin to roam, but they only rarely come to central or western Europe in winter, and then it is generally when there is a shortage of larch cones in the north. They are sometimes found alone, and at other times in flocks with the Common Crossbill. Invasions of the Two-barred Crossbill are rare and irregular. The Two-barred Crossbill is an inhabitant of the far north, mainly of western Siberia, the northern part of North America and northern Europe where it occurs from northern Sweden across to the Urals (1).

1

It resembles the Common Crossbill in structure, behaviour and coloration. It has a finer bill, with the lower mandible elongated and raised and better adapted for opening larch cones. The main distinctive feature of the Two-barred Crossbill is a pair of broad white bars across the wing, present both in the red-coloured males (3) and the yellowish females (2). In flight they look not unlike Chaffinches.

A third species, the Parrot Crossbill *(Loxia pytyopsittacus)* lives in the pine forests of northern Europe and has a very stout bill. The three species demonstrate

2 ♀

3 ♂

the adaptation of beak shape to their
most frequent food: Parrot Crossbill (4)
— pine seeds; Common Crossbill (5) —
spruce seeds; Two-barred Crossbill (6) —
larch seeds.

4

5

6

Hawfinch
Coccothraustes coccothraustes

Fringillidae

The most outstanding feature of the Hawfinch is its massive bill, which is adapted for cracking fruit stones. Hawfinches pick the fruit on trees, tear off the pulp and throw it away and then crack the stone and take out the kernel. They are usually hidden in the treetops and their presence is often betrayed only by the snapping of stones. They also feed on other seeds with tough coats, and, when these are not available, on the seeds of weeds, apples, pears, etc. The young are regularly fed on insects. The Hawfinch's favourite haunts are deciduous mixed woods and parks; it also frequents old gardens and fruit orchards, mainly cherry orchards. Hawfinches begin to build their nests in April, generally in deciduous trees. The nest is a fairly large construction, although its size comes from the strong, long twigs of deciduous trees sticking out of the base. Other materials include rootlets, stalks and moss. The cup is made of fine rootlets, sometimes of horsehair and hairs. The female lays four to six bluish, brown-speckled eggs with dark dots and lines and mainly sits on them alone, although the male occasionally relieves her. In 14 days the young hatch, and grow up in another 14 days before leaving the nest. The adults keep them company for a long time; there is no second clutch. Most Hawfinches from central Europe fly southwards for the winter, and northern Hawfinches take their places. The birds from more southerly regions are resident.

2

Although the Hawfinch is conspicuous with its large head and stout, conical beak, it is not an easy bird to see. It lives mainly in the treetops and many people do not know it well by sight. Usually, it attracts attention by its sharp calls — 'tsiks-tsiks'. The male has a black patch around the beak and on the throat, glossy black wings with a broad white wingbar and a white tip to the tail. The neck is grey, but the bird is mainly brown in colour: it is buffish on the head, rump and underparts and darker brown above. From about March to July the beak is grey-blue, becoming brownish (1) for the

1 ♂

rest of the year. The female has duller colours. The young lack the black head pattern; the throat is pale and the breast is covered by brown spots. The gape in nestlings is very colourful — blue, purple and red (2). The fifth to ninth primaries have a special shape: they look as if they

4

3

have been cut crosswise, and are elongated at the end of the outer web, while the inner web has a rounded edge (3). The Hawfinch occurs all over Europe (north to southern Scandinavia), in north Africa and Asia and in a belt south of the coniferous taiga east to Japan (4).

189

Bullfinch
Pyrrhula pyrrhula

If you know how to imitate the sad, quiet 'dee-dee' of the Bullfinch, you can easily attract a whole flock. Bullfinches are extremely gregarious and immediately follow the call. The northern birds are even more confiding. Bullfinches pair early in spring, arriving at their nesting grounds in March, already in pairs, and in April the female begins to build the nest. It is a flat construction of freely superimposed twigs at the base, on to which the female builds a cup of fine rootlets, lichens and hairs. The eggs are pale blue with greyish cloud-like markings and black-brown dots and streaks, averaging four to five in a clutch. The chicks hatch in 13 to 15 days, leaving the nest 12 to 15 days later. The eggs are incubated only by the female; the male guards her and brings food. Both then look after the young and feed them on insects and seeds. Most pairs breed once more, in June or July. In temperate areas Bullfinches are resident or roam near their nesting territories. Northern Bullfinches move out and winter far to the south. At that time, they feed only on the seeds of various plants and trees, pecking off tree buds. The Bullfinch seeks mixed woods with abundant bushy undergrowth, and in the mountains even coniferous forests. It is also quite happy with thickets around brooks and bush-covered slopes, or old large parks, orchards, cemeteries and gardens.

4

The Bullfinch is somewhat larger and more robust than the Sparrow. The male is conspicuous with red underparts between a black chin and the white under tail coverts. The head has a black cap extending below the eyes, and the tail and wings are also black, the latter with a white wingbar. The mantle is grey (1). In flight the Bullfinch can be recognized by its white rump (2). The female has a similar pattern, but the red is replaced by a duller grey-brown (3). Juveniles are uniform rust-brown, lacking the black cap. The gape of nestlings is a combination of crimson and purplish

2 ♂

1 ♂

3 ♀

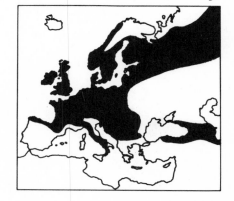

5

pigments (4). It is interesting that the female Bullfinch also sings, but the male delivers a better and louder song. The Bullfinch ranges almost all over Europe, except in the southernmost and northernmost areas, and in a broad belt in Asia north of the Himalayas east to Japan (5).

Tree Sparrow
Passer montanus

Passeridae

The name 'Sparrow' usually suggests the House Sparrow. Most people know only vaguely if at all about the existence of another species — the Tree Sparrow. It is hardly ever seen in the middle of cities — in rare cases just in parks or gardens with old trees. The Tree Sparrow prefers open country with overgrown areas rich in old hollow trees, e.g. forest edges, lines of old roadside trees and thickets along streams — it is much more dependent on greenery and 'natural' habitats than the House Sparrow. It nests in holes in trees and walls and in nestboxes, but also in the bases of Storks' or Eagles' nests, in Sand Martins' holes, etc. The pair stuff the hole with lots of straw, hay, wool, papers, rags and hairs, creating a conical, untidy 'Sparrow's nest' with a soft lining of feathers. Exceptionally the birds build a nest on a tree. The female lays five to six eggs up to three times a year. Both parents share the incubation for 13 to 14 days. In another 14 to 16 days the young are fledged and can leave the nest. The adults feed them chiefly on insects which form the mainstay of their diet; the chicks also eat seeds, buds and fruits. After fledging Tree Sparrows gather in flocks and roam the fields, roosting in thick treetops, bushes or reeds. Pairs remain together at that time. In winter the Tree Sparrow, unlike the House Sparrow, joins flocks of other seedeaters — Buntings, Chaffinches, Bramblings, etc. Some pairs stay in their nesting territories, sleeping in old, well-lined nests. Exceptionally, a mixed pair of the Tree Sparrow and the House Sparrow can be formed. The Tree Sparrow inhabits almost all of Europe, Asia and north Africa.

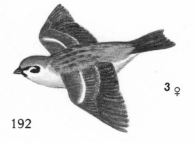

3 ♀

Although the Tree Sparrow resembles the House Sparrow, they can be distinguished easily by an attentive observer. The Tree Sparrow is smaller, with a chestnut-brown crown (the House Sparrow has a wide ash-grey band (1) on the crown), separated from the streaked back by a white collar. The white cheeks

2 ♂

4

1

have a half-moon black patch, while the chin and the bridle-like strip from the eye to the beak (2, 3) are also black. The female is identical to the male, but the young are duller in appearance. The Tree Sparrow is an active and restless bird, constantly hopping around and flicking its tail. It moves briskly on the ground and makes short rapid flights, or sometimes longer ones, in an undulating manner. The eggs are variable in colour, but the ground colour is usually grey-green, covered by dense dark spots (4).

193

Common Starling
Sturnus vulgaris

Sturnidae

The Common Starling is one of the earliest heralds of spring. If it has gone away (which it does not always do in Britain) it returns in February or March. Starlings stay in flocks at first, but as soon as the weather improves the males turn up at nestboxes and cavities, singing with half-spread wings and open bills. They are found anywhere where nestboxes and holes are available. They are very adaptable and do not exclusively require natural tree cavities, but will nest also in holes in walls or rocks. They readily use man-made nestboxes, which have certainly contributed to the vast expansion of Starlings. They originated in deciduous woods where they used to nest in hollow trees and find food in meadows or grassland. The nest is built by the female, although her mate helps to bring in the material. The nest is made of straw, dry grass, twigs, and a lot of feathers. The four to six beautiful green-blue eggs are incubated by the female at night and by both partners in the daytime. The young hatch in 14 days, and leave the nest some 18 to 22 days later. From the age of 14 days, they accept food from the adults, rattling loudly at the entrance. A few pairs breed once more in June or July. In August and September, flocks of thousands of Starlings gather to spend the nights in reed-beds or treetops until the October departure for southern Europe. Some Starlings winter in central Europe; in Britain vast numbers roost in big cities in winter. Starlings have a characteristic torpedo shape in flight. They feed mainly on animal life such as insects, worms, small molluscs and spiders during the breeding season; from late summer they consume plant food — various seeds and fruit.

Both sexes are basically black, with a beautiful metallic sheen. The individual feathers are white-tipped (1), but these tips wear off gradually throughout spring, so that by June the Starling is almost uniformly black (2). From July the black plumage starts moulting and is replaced by streaked feathers. The bill also changes colour from the yellow of spring and summer to brown in autumn and winter. The first plumage of the juveniles is grey-brown. The Starling is an agile, gregarious bird which tends to live in colonies. People partly dislike it for the damage it can cause in vineyards and fruit orchards, but otherwise are fond of it, as can be seen from the provision of nestboxes, and from the fact that emigrants took it with them to North America, south Africa, Australia and to New Zealand. The history of the North American distribution is particularly

194

interesting: in the years 1890-91, one hundred Starlings were set free from cages in the middle of New York. For six years they stayed in the city, but then began to spread so rapidly that in 70 years they flooded the United States, and now nest even in Alaska (3). This is proof of the enormous adaptability and fertility of Starlings.

In America they are represented by some 100 species of Icterids (Icteridae), resembling Starlings in many properties.

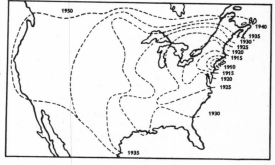

Golden Oriole
Oriolus oriolus

The Golden Oriole is the only European representative of the tropical family of Oriolidae. At present, it inhabits Europe south of Scandinavia, across to south-western Siberia. It also lives in parts of north-western Africa and in Asia Minor. Its tropical origin makes it a strictly migratory bird which is present in central Europe for a short time only in summer. The Golden Oriole is among the last migrants to arrive, usually in the first days of May. It breeds in old parks, orchards, avenues of trees and brushwood along streams where there are sufficiently tall trees, and frequents deciduous woods and sometimes pine woods. It avoids dark coniferous forests. Despite the beautiful and striking colours of the Golden Oriole it is only rarely seen in the open. It is shy and wary, and almost always stays in the thick foliage of tall trees, where it also constructs its nest. The clutch contains three to five white eggs with a small number of black or black-brown dots. Both partners share in the incubation, but the female undertakes the major part. The young hatch after 14 to 15 days, leaving the nest in a further 2 weeks. The diet is mainly insects, captured on the wing or picked up in trees, and spiders and small gastropods. Plants are added at the end of summer when the Oriole eats soft fruits such as cherries, mulberries, pears and various berries. From August, Orioles begin to set out on their long journey to tropical Africa.

2 ♀

3

1 ♂

The male has two basic colours: the wings, the centre of the tail and a bridle-like stripe from the beak to the eye are black; the rest is bright golden-yellow. These colours are strikingly complemented by the crimson-red eyes and the red-brown beak (1). The female is yellow-green above; the rump is a richer yellow and the underparts are yellowish-white with darker streaks. The black colour of males is replaced by grey-brown (2), the young are similarly coloured. The Golden Oriole's nest is immediately recognizable: it is a basket of leaves and the stalks of grasses, plant and bark fibres and bark chips, lined with soft grasses, wool and feathers, tied with bark and other long fibres into a horizontal fork of thin outer branches (3). The Golden Oriole is a restless bird and often flies from one tree to another, which is when it is usually seen. The spring arrival is announced by the male's loud, flute-like whistling 'litilidee-o'. The male is a very persistent songster, repeating his song for hours on end. A shrill, high-pitched 'kraack' sometimes unexpectedly follows the soft flute-like tune. The Golden Oriole is very fond of bathing: a bright yellow male, swooping down to the water surface in a Swallow-like manner, is a beautiful sight.

Jay
Garrulus glandarius

Corvidae

The Jay is a sort of forest policeman: it is exceedingly cautious and its harsh croaking warns all the inhabitants of the forest that man is approaching long before he can sight it. The Jay is a typical forest-dweller: it is found in all types of woodland, preferably in old mixed woods, but also in field groves or large old parks. From April both members of the pair begin to build a nest in a treetop. They choose both conifers and deciduous trees, and often seek stands of spruce close to forest edges. The nest is relatively small and flat; the outer layer is made of twigs, the interior of dry grass and rootlets. When five to eight eggs have accumulated in the nest the clutch is complete. Both partners participate in the incubation, which begins after the laying of the first egg and lasts for 16 to 17 days. They react to the slightest disturbance, often deserting the clutch. Some three weeks after the hatch, the young are so independent that they can leave the nest and wander off with their parents. The Jay consumes both vegetable and animal food, the latter chiefly in the breeding period; the young feed on various invertebrates, but are also brought small vertebrates such as voles and small birds. By preying on birds' nests and eating both eggs and nestlings, the Jay has earned the reputation of being one of the greatest predators of small birds. The plant diet is important later in the year and consists of acorns, beech nuts, hazel nuts and berries. The Jay occurs all over Europe, in north Africa and Asia (except its southern regions). It is predominantly a resident bird but Jays from the north and north-east sometimes gather in large flocks and migrate far to the south and south-west.

3

198

Both sexes have the same, overall pink-grey coloration (1). The black-and-white feathers on the crown form a small erectile crest. An elongated black stripe extends downwards from the lower mandible in the form of a moustache. The tail is black, in striking contrast to the white rump. The upper wing coverts are the most outstanding feathers: they are a vivid blue with dark bars and often with white lines in between — the well-known 'Jay feathers' (2). There is a large white patch in the wings. In the young the plumage is somewhat darker and not so colourful. The Jay avoids open spaces and prefers to fly from one tree to another. It hops clumsily on the ground. Its vocal repertoire is very varied: it can imitate various sounds and the voices of other birds.

In North America, the European Jay species are represented by the genus *Cyanocorax* and *Cyanocitta* (3), the so-called Blue Jays. In their way of life they do not differ very much from our Jays.

199

Magpie
Pica pica

Corvidae

The Magpie is a well-known corvid with its black-and-white plumage and long, graduated tail. It is hardly likely to be mistaken for any other species. Its large nest is very characteristic and original. The top is covered by a thorny roof, the base is of dry twigs, the middle layer is of mud and sods and the upper one is of rootlets, stalks, leaves and hairs. The Magpie's nest is situated high in the treetops whenever possible, but otherwise is also built in bushes. Magpies usually build several nests, and later select one of them. In April or May, five to eight eggs appear in the nest; they are brown-speckled on a brownish or greenish ground colour. The female incubates for 17 to 18 days. The male does not participate, but helps his mate with the feeding of the ever-hungry young. The young remain in the nest for 22 to 27 days, then fly out and roam the neighbourhood. Only one brood is reared in a summer. The Magpie is not too gregarious, living usually in single pairs, or in families for some time after the young fledge. In places where Magpies are plentiful, however, they sometimes gather into larger parties in autumn and use communal roosts. The Magpie is sedentary and never roams too far in autumn or in winter; even young Magpies start families near the site where they were born. The diet is varied: in the nesting period Magpies rob the nests of other birds or consume small mammals, insects, molluscs and other animals, various berries, fruit, corn, etc.

With its distinctive shape, movements and plumage, the Magpie (1) is a very conspicuous bird. If it hops on the ground, it bobs its raised tail, which is longer than

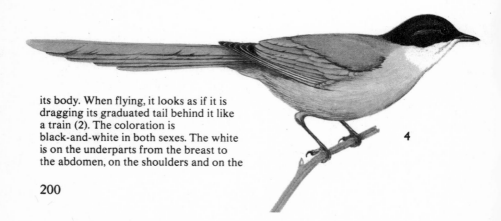

its body. When flying, it looks as if it is dragging its graduated tail behind it like a train (2). The coloration is black-and-white in both sexes. The white is on the underparts from the breast to the abdomen, on the shoulders and on the

4

agricultural lands where trees and bushes
are plentiful, but avoiding continuous
forests. It is distributed throughout
Europe, Asia, north Africa and North
America (3), where there is also
a yellow-billed magpie species — *Pica
nuttalli.*

The Iberian Peninsula is the home of
the Azure-winged Magpie *Cyanopica
cyana* (4), which is interesting mainly
because of its curious distribution. It lives
in Spain and Portugal and in eastern Asia.

inner webs of primaries. The rest of the
body is black with a beautiful green, blue
and purple gloss. Juveniles have shorter
tails and all the black areas lack the
lustrous sheen. The Magpie can also be
recognized easily by its voice, a harsh,
rattling 'tcha-tcha-tcha'. It has
a reputation for stealing and hiding shiny
objects. The Magpie inhabits open

201

Nutcracker
Nucifraga caryocatactes

The Nutcracker was originally a bird of the taiga. It occurs in a continuous, broad belt from Scandinavia through Siberia to Japan. In Europe it also occurs in isolated spots in mountainous coniferous forests. Recently, it has been spreading into continuous coniferous woodlands at lower altitudes. It begins to construct its nest in March, when the forests are still covered by snow. The building is undertaken by both partners, most frequently in the thick branches of coniferous trees, usually close to the trunk. Nutcrackers break off twigs, often fresh ones, and arrange them as a base. This is followed by a characteristic layer of rotting wood, sometimes combined with lichens; the lining is of dry grass, moss and occasionally feathers. The clutch numbers three to five eggs; these are greenish and covered by brown spots. The female incubates them alone for 16 to 18 days, while the male feeds her. The rearing of the nestlings takes 23 to 25 days; it is undertaken by both parents. After fledging, the young remain with the adults. The Nutcracker eats mainly vegetable food: it is fond of mountain-pine nuts, the seeds of other conifers, beech nuts, hazel nuts and acorns. It holds nuts with its feet and breaks them open with the beak. Nutcrackers also eat insects and worms, and occasionally prey on nestlings or eggs. Like other corvids, Nutcrackers hide seeds in caches. They have a good memory and often find most of their stores. They are largely resident, but move southwards in autumn and winter, or descend from the mountains to places where they have never been seen before, even to city parks and gardens, where they search for hazel nuts.

The Nutcracker is a very quiet bird; its presence often goes unnoticed. Its voice resembles that of the Jay: it produces a grating 'kerr-kerr' sound, most frequently heard from treetops in spring. It is smaller than the Jay, but has a longer, stouter beak. Both sexes are identically coloured, rich brown with drop-like white spots, absent only on the crown, wings and tail. The tail is terminated by a white band (1). The young are markedly paler, with fewer white spots.

Europe is inhabited by the European Nutcracker *(Nucifraga caryocatactes caryocatactes)*, with a strong, short beak and a narrow (15 to 25 mm) white band at the end of the tail.

The Siberian Nutcracker *(Nucifraga*

caryocatactes macrorhynchos) is found in the Siberian taiga, and occurs in Europe during invasions caused by a shortage of mountain-pine seeds, its main diet. It has a narrower and longer beak, and a wider (25 to 33 mm) white band on the tail. The coniferous forests of North America are the home of the related species *Nucifraga columbiana* (2).

Rook
Corvus frugilegus

The Rook is a characteristic bird of open country in winter. During the day they forage for food in fields, meadows, and even in towns; in the evening, they leave by a common route and go to communal roosts; on the following day, in the darkness before dawn, they fly out again in a wide radius to search for food. The numerous flocks stay approximately from October to March, when Rooks gradually depart: birds from central Europe move westwards to locations with resident or transient populations. The Rook is resident in Europe in a broad belt from Britain and France, northern Italy, Yugoslavia and Romania, to the Baltic and a vast part of Asia. The Rook prefers an open landscape in lowlands, with large fields and meadows, scattered groves, groups of trees or thickets along streams; it also nests at forest margins or in city parks and cemeteries. The Rook usually nests in colonies: one tree can contain several dozen nests, which sometimes almost touch one another. In March, Rooks repair old nests or build new ones of broken twigs, mud, moss, rootlets and dry grass. Both partners carry out the construction, but one of them has to stay at the building site as the nest nears completion, since materials are constantly stolen by other Rooks. The nest soon contains three to five greenish, brown-speckled eggs; the female incubates them for 17 to 19 days while the male regularly brings her food. He continues to do this in the first days after hatching when the female does not leave the young too often. Both parents later set out to hunt for food, bringing it back in the special throat pouch. The rearing of the nestlings takes 30 to 35 days. The diet is highly varied: insects, worms, gastropods, small mammals, often carrion, various types of corn, remains of potatoes, berries, etc.

3

Most people call these black birds Crows. They are, however, distinguished from Crows by a strong purplish-blue gloss; in adult Rooks, the whitish bare skin around the base of the beak (1) is distinct; the young, until they are a year old, have the base covered by normal feathers (2). The Rook has other distinctive features: the slender and more elongated bill and 'trousers' — shaggy feathers covering the

2

1

legs. A feather from the crown is broad,
with a rounded end (3). Both sexes look
alike. When walking, Rooks move with
a pronounced waddling gait. They are
good, efficient fliers: if they nest in the
centre of a city they can easily fly out to
their foraging grounds several kilometres
away. Disgorged remains of food can be
found in their sleeping quarters, revealing
the composition of their diet.

Crow
Corvus corone

The Crow frequents all kinds of open country, as well as forest margins and groves among fields and pastures; it also nests in city centres. It never breeds in colonies like the Rook, always in single pairs. The courtship takes place on warm February or March days, and pairs seem to stay together for life. The nest is built by both partners high in a treetop; the base is made of broken dry twigs, mud and moss; the cup is lined with hairs and grass. The clutch contains four to six eggs, resembling Rook's eggs, and the female incubates them alone and very assiduously. She leaves the nest only when taking food brought by the male (he will also feed her while she is on the nest), or when taking a short flight. The young hatch after 17 to 20 days; the female sits on them at first, but after a week joins the male in bringing them food. The young are mature some 4 to 5 weeks later, and can leave the nest and roam the environs with their parents, probably until winter. Northern Crows may fly as far south as central Europe. Crows are omnivorous, although they prefer animal food. They consume everything from insects, small birds and mammals to carrion; they prey on birds' eggs on a large scale, usually 'sucking' the eggs. They also eat grain, the green parts of plants, fruits etc.

The Crow is a very cautious and shrewd bird (however, this does not apply to Hoodies, living in the east, in towns — these are extraordinarily intrusive and impudent). In winter, Crows sometimes join flocks of Rooks and Jackdaws.

Two races of Crow live in Europe (4). The Carrion Crow inhabits the western part of Europe, approximately to the Elbe and the Moldau, then towards Vienna and across the Alps to northern Italy. The Hooded Crow (2) is distributed to the north and east, far into eastern Siberia. Both occur in a wide zone of overlap, which leads to the formation of pairs with one black (Carrion) and one grey (Hooded) Crow. Hybrids produced from the mixed pairs are blacker than the average Hooded Crows.

3

The Carrion Crow *(Corvus corone corone)* is completely black with a greenish and purplish sheen (1); the Hooded Crow *(Corvus corone cornix)* has a black head, throat, wings, tail and thighs; the rest is grey (2). Males and

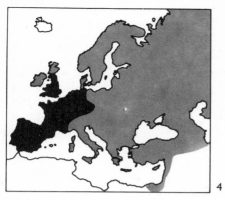

females in both subspecies look alike. The
Carrion Crow can often be mistaken for
a young Rook, but the experienced
observer can recognize it by its more
massive, deeper beak, slightly curved
along the upper ridge, and by the colour
of its gloss. It has narrow and pointed
feathers on the crown (3).

In North America, the Crow is
represented by the species *Corvus
brachyrhynchos,* the American Crow.

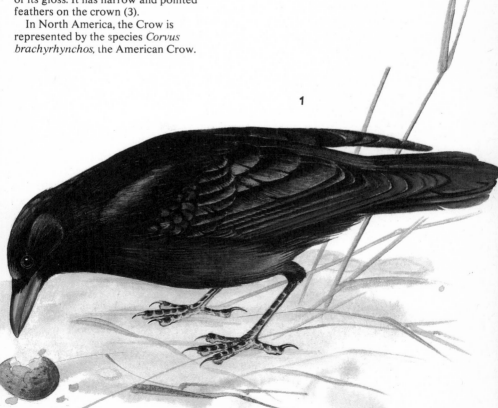

Migration of songbirds

Turning to changes in the areas where birds live in the course of the year, songbirds can be divided into migratory, transient and resident. The migratory birds have in fact two homes: one in the north, where they rear their young, and one in the southern winter quarters, where they never breed. They include virtually all the insectivorous passerine birds, which avoid the winter shortage of food by migrating. The resident birds remain faithful to one site all their life, and do not leave it in the non-breeding period, e.g. the Nuthatch and the Crested Tit. A transition between the two groups is formed by transient birds, which roam in winter in a large radius around the nesting ground, sometimes to distances of a hundred or more kilometres. They include various seedeaters: Goldfinches, Greenfinches or Linnets. There are also songbirds which appear in certain areas only once in a few years, but in large numbers. They are so-called 'invasion' birds, constituting a specific category. Invasions have been observed in Crossbills, Siberian Nutcrackers, Waxwings and Lesser Redpolls. Invasions are usually sparked off by poor harvests of certain seeds in an extensive home territory of these birds, or provoked by overbreeding of birds, unfavourable weather, etc.

A lot has been written about the speed of a bird's migratory flight, but it is generally over-estimated. The travelling speed of the Hooded Crow is 50 km p.h., in Chaffinch-type birds 52.5 km p.h., in Jackdaws 61.5 km p.h., and in the Starling 74.1 km p.h. The height of the flight is not too remarkable either: small birds usually migrate at a height up to 100 metres, Starlings up to 50 or 100 metres, and Crows from 30 to 200 metres.

Songbirds migrate more or less everywhere, over a wide front which occasionally narrows into 'corridors', e.g. in mountainous valleys or in coastal areas. The birds do not fly in a fixed formation, but in an apparently disorganized flock, as seen for instance in Starlings or Chaffinches. Another group of songbirds is composed of birds migrating individually (Golden Oriole, Red-backed Shrike). Many birds migrate at night and escape attention. It is interesting that the night flights are undertaken by many species that otherwise live in the daytime, e.g. larks, thrushes, Robins or warblers. The night flight probably provides some advantages; they are secure from raptors and can use the day for the collection of food and for resting.

Many songbirds arrive in spring at a specific time; the majority of birds scatter over a certain area within four to ten days of the arrival of the major group. Songbirds noted for such regularity of arrival include the Swallow, the warblers and many other species. Among the early-arriving birds are the Wheatear or the Chiffchaff, returning to the nesting grounds at the end of March. Some insectivorous birds, or birds requiring perfect cover in tops of deciduous trees, arrive very late: e.g. in Europe, Golden Orioles, Icterine Warblers or Red-backed Shrikes, all of which winter in faraway equatorial Africa. The males generally arrive earlier to occupy the nesting territories; the females follow them.

The departure for winter quarters is less regular: it may take place soon after the rearing of the young (Flycatchers), or it may be protracted. In some species with a strong migratory instinct, the young set out on their first journey to the south independently (Red-backed Shrike).

Songbirds and man

The economic importance of some birds is undoubtedly considerable when one considers the vast markets for poultry and their eggs. If songbirds can generally be said to be of economic importance it is through their effect on insects which damage crops. However, their value in this 'biological warfare' against insect pests is often overstated. Although there is no doubt that certain songbirds such as warblers and tits consume large quantities of insects, these birds cannot 'control' the numbers of their prey species as it is the numbers of the prey which effectively determine the numbers of predators. However, in one instance, it has been discovered that there was a noticeable decrease in the amount of damage caused by cockchafers in the vicinity of a rookery. On the other hand, the passerines include some species which can be an agricultural pest; for example large flocks of Starlings have been known to damage cornfields and Bullfinches, in some areas, have been accused of damaging orchard crops. It is difficult to ascertain the exact importance of various species, as their diet often changes with the time of year and even with the locality. Because of this no bird can be called purely useful or harmful from man's point of view. It is important, however, not to justify the protection of birds only by the economic interests of man; it should be a cultural and aesthetic decision as well.

Songbird populations

Numbers of birds are subject to considerable annual differences — tits are a well-known case in point. These short term changes are brought about by various conditions, many of them are so far not fully explored. These conditions include climatic factors in the nesting territories, wintering grounds or during migration, such as heavy rain or unfavourable winds. The west European population of Whitethroats suffered heavy losses during the late 60's and early 70's as a result of a severe drought in the Sahel region south of the Sahara where the population regularly winters. As a result of this the breeding population in Britain dropped by 77 % in 1969 compared with the previous year despite a productive breeding season in 1968 and favourable climatic conditions during the migration.

Apart from natural hazards songbirds migrating from northern Europe through countries like France and Italy have to face an army of 'sportsmen' who still shoot birds such as Skylarks, thrushes, buntings and finches for sport and for food. Many are also caught for sale as caged birds. This means that for successful protection of some birds it is important that international agreement is reached.

The local distribution of songbirds in Europe is often dependent on the land use and here large scale agricultural practices have effectively reduced the amount of habitat suitable for a wide variety of species. In order to maximize productivity enormous single purpose fields have been created leaving a landscape empty of hedges. Areas of marshland have been drained, copses and woodland have been destroyed, brooks have been replaced by barren dykes. Mixed deciduous woodland with its wide variety of nest sites and feeding niches has been replaced by monotonous coniferous forests which support a much smaller range of wildlife but give a much more profitable yield to the forester. For example, in the uniform spruce forests the only abundant species are perhaps Coal Tits, Goldcrests and Chaffinches. In the immense field systems the only bird likely to be encountered is the Skylark. But as soon as you come to a copse or an established hedge other species can be found such as warblers, Linnets, Greenfinches, Wrens and other songbirds. The smaller mixed farms support a much wider spectrum of bird species because of the mosaic of different biotypes, where fields and meadows are combined with woods and water surfaces. This variety does not mean that there is just an increase in the numbers of breeding birds but the various habitats provide important haunts for birds throughout the year.

The formation of large areas of land almost entirely devoted to agriculture and the need for increasingly intensive farming has meant that the delicate natural balance of the land has been lost. In order to maintain the fertility of soil and control the insect populations, chemical fertilizers and insecticides have been used. The application of these substances is nowadays common practice over enormous areas, as is forest dusting with insecticides. The artificial control of the insect population has had a dramatic effect on species higher up in the food chain. In the early 1960s vast numbers of birds were found to have been killed due to the uncontrolled use of some of these insecticides (particularly DDT, Dieldrin, Aldrin and Heptachlor). In parts of the United States the effects of these chemicals were severe. For example, areas covered by elms were sprayed with insecticides for a disease spread by insects. The DDT penetrated the ground and then the earthworms, which were resistant to it but deposited the chemicals in their tissues. Thrushes, consuming the earthworms, gradually built up the DDT in their system and eventually it became so great that they became paralyzed and died. The mortality rate of thrushes like the American Robin reached as high as 86 % in some populations. An estimated 10,000 birds died of mercurial poisoning in one 80-acre field. Parathion, a highly toxic organophosphorous compound which is still used in some tropical areas, although it has been largely withdrawn elsewhere, killed more than 200,000 birds of 55 different species in Holland in 1960. These chemicals are largely banned now in temperate countries.

Insecticides often provoke serious physiological disturbances mainly in the reproductive organs. They can cause partial or total sterility resulting in diminished or infertile clutches. Insecticides can also affect the deposition of calcium in egg-shells causing them to become soft or fragile and break easily. The effect on the breeding success of raptors is best known but these effects have been observed in many passerines as well.

Bird protection and conservation

The conservation of birds does not merely consist of the passive preservation of individual species. It should also include the use of active management of certain environments so that the best is achieved both in terms of providing suitable habitats and allowing man to use the land.

In many countries the present-day landscape is characterized by a loss of suitable nest sites for birds, such as hedgerows and old decaying trees. This can sometimes be offset by providing artificial nest sites in the form of nest boxes. Species such as tits, redstarts and flycatchers which would normally nest in cavities will often use these. There are now many different types and shapes of nest box which can provide sites for a wide range of birds from Kestrels and Tawny Owls to Swifts and House Martins. Instructions on how to make these boxes or where to buy them can be found in most general books on birdwatching. It is important to remember that most birds require a specific territory when they are nesting so it would be wasteful to place nest boxes close to each other. The minimum distance apart in deciduous or mixed woods should be approximately 25 metres; in coniferous forest or scrub about 50 metres.

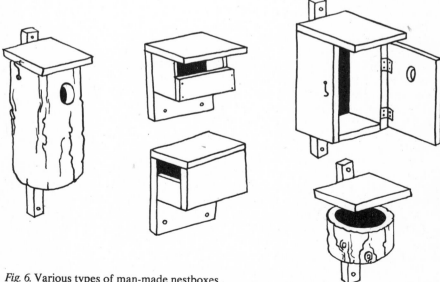

Fig. 6. Various types of man-made nestboxes

211

However, the most effective method of providing nest sites is by the maintenance of a suitable habitat which has sufficient cover at all levels. For example, although several warblers feed in the upper branches of trees, where they catch small insects, they nest in the understorey of the wood so it is important that cover is maintained at both levels. Another useful aid is the provision of 'nesting-pockets' (Fig. 7) on tree trunks. These are bunches of pine (with long-lasting needles or a thick portion of bush fastened to the tree with a wire or a rope. The thinner end of the branch is tied to the trunk, while the stronger ones are bent in an arc upwards and then fastened. A cavity is then formed, in which a suitable hollow is made which may prove inviting to thrushes, Greenfinches, Linnets, Wrens and other small birds.

During the winter the feeding of birds from garden bird-tables often provides important extra-food for small birds especially during periods of hard weather. It is possible to buy seeds and nuts for this purpose and some household scraps are also suitable. It is best if the bird-table is at least a metre from the ground in order to stop cats and squirrels from getting at them. The wooden support can be covered with a length of plastic piping to make it more difficult for these animals to climb up. It is important also to clean the bird table from time to time to avoid the risk of *Salmonella* infection. The feeding of birds in the garden apart from helping the birds to survive through particularly hard weather also provides a wonderful opportunity to study the habits of some of the commoner songbirds.

Fig. 7. A nesting pocket

Index of Common Names

Index of Scientific Names

216